CROWS

ENCOUNTERS WITH THE WISE GUYS

OF THE AVIAN WORLD

CANDACE SAVAGE

CROWS

GREYSTONE BOOKS
Douglas & McIntyre Publishing Group
Vancouver / Toronto / Berkeley

05 06 07 08 09   5 4 3 2 1

Greystone Books

A division of Douglas & McIntyre Ltd.

2323 Quebec Street, Suite 201

Vancouver, British Columbia

Canada V5T 4S7

www.greystonebooks.com

Library and Archives Canada Cataloguing in Publication

Savage, Candace, date.

Crows : encounters with the wise guys of the avian world / Candace Savage.

Includes bibliographical references and index.

ISBN-13: 978-1-55365-106-2   ISBN-10: 1-55365-106-5

1. Crows. 2. Ravens. I. Title.

QL696.P23675293 2005   598.8'64   C2005-902131-4

Library of Congress Cataloging-in-Publication Data available upon request

Editing by Nancy Flight

Jacket and text design by Jessica Sullivan

Jacket illustrations by Tony Angell

Printed and bound in China by C&C Offset Printing Co., Ltd.

Printed on acid-free paper

Distributed in the U.S. by Publishers Group West

We gratefully acknowledge the financial support of the Canada Council for the Arts,
the British Columbia Arts Council, and the Government of Canada through the Book
Publishing Industry Development Program (BPIDP) for our publishing activities.

{ CONTENTS }

✦   ✦   ✦

The Crow

CONNECTION

✦   ✦   ✦

LIKE MOST PEOPLE, I have crow stories to tell.
There was the time in the northern forest
when a raven—and what is a raven except a
crow taken to the extreme?—flew over my head, looked down, uttered a
rasping call, and then made two complete barrel rolls before continuing
smoothly on. "I am a raven," it seemed to say, "and you, poor thing, are not."
There was the American crow, glimpsed through a car window just outside
the city where I live, that was hanging by its beak from a branch and whipping around in the wind. More than anything, there is the everyday pleasure

➤ *Birds of a feather flock together in this engraving of four crows and one crow*
cousin. In the midground, from left to right, are the jackdaw, rook, and carrion crow and
the related black-billed magpie. In front, a common raven picks at a dead rabbit.

of seeing those lithe, calling forms rowing through the air, bound for somewhere. Any day with a crow in it is full of promise.

Admittedly, not everyone shares this enthusiasm for wild black wings. To some folks, crows and their kin—the ravens, jackdaws, and rooks—are nothing but a darned nuisance. Where a more sympathetic observer might appreciate the birds' role as scavengers (nature's clean-up crew), these people are disgusted by a diet that includes the dead and the rotten. Where you or I might hear an interesting confusion of crow voices, these others hear only noise. And where a thoughtful person might reflect on the intricate relationship between predator and prey, the crows' detractors are alarmed by their depredations on songbirds. In this connection, it is worth noting that although crows do feed on eggs and nestlings, there is no evidence that these losses have reduced songbird numbers. Alas, the same cannot be said for the endangered desert tortoise of the southwestern United States, which is being battered by a burgeoning population of garbage-fed ravens.

Happily, for every person who views crows with distrust, there is someone who enjoys and appreciates them. One of the many delights of writing this book has been making contact with this growing flock of corvid enthusiasts. Who knew that there was a lively online community of crow people in various parts of the world, all busily tap-tap-tapping out their stories and sharing them with one another? Did you hear about the raven that dropped a crumpled-up bag on a kid who was holding an order of fries? Or how about

the crows that, day after day, singled out a particular factory worker on his lunch break in a parking lot and treated him to intense displays of bowing and rattlelike calls? All this and much more is just a mouse-click away at sites like those listed on page 107.

But this book is not just a celebration of day-to-day encounters with these fascinating birds. My aim is to delve deeper. The information in these pages derives primarily from a decade and more of systematic and often audacious research by leading scientists in three major regions: Europe, North America, and Australasia. It has been my privilege to speak with many of these experts and to hear firsthand about their discoveries, some of which have not previously been published. In particular, it is an honor to acknowledge

◄ *Crows are generalists, with a keen interest
in all things edible. This engraving, by R. Havell,
is based on a drawing by John J. Audubon.*

the assistance of Vittorio Baglione, University of Seville, Spain; Thomas Bugnyar, Konrad Lorenz Research Station, University of Vienna, Austria; Anne Clark, University of Binghamton, USA; Nicky Clayton, Cambridge University, England; Peter Enggist, Enggist Science Consulting, Switzerland; Sylvia Hope, California Academy of Sciences, USA; Gavin Hunt, University of Auckland, New Zealand; Alex Kacelnik, Oxford University, England; John Marzluff, University of Washington, USA; Kevin McGowan, Cornell Laboratory of Ornithology, USA; Cynthia Sims Parr, University of Maryland Institute for Advanced Computer Studies, USA; and Daniel Stahler, Yellowstone Center for Resources, Yellowstone National Park, USA. Bernd Heinrich of the University of Vermont was interviewed for an article entitled "Reasoning Ravens" that was published in *Canadian Geographic* in 2000. John Spirko of Fort Erie, Ontario, and Sandy Harbanuk of the Juneau Raptor Center are among those who shared their stories with me; Barbara Hodgson provided the fine illustration that appears on page 17. A special word of thanks is due to Dr. Carolee Caffrey, until recently the West Nile virus specialist for the National Audubon Society, USA, for her enthusiasm, knowledge, and generosity.

Crow lovers one and all, these busy people found time not only to answer my many questions but also, in several cases, to review relevant portions of the text. I am grateful for their collaboration and, most of all, for their crow-like fascination with the world around them.

The Birds in
B L A C K

❖   ❖   ❖

O N A N I S L A N D in the South Pacific Ocean, somewhere west of Fiji, a sleek black crow is poking around in the greenery of a sun-streaked rain forest. With its senses sharply focused on the search for food, the bird hops from branch to branch and from plant to plant, jabbing its stout beak into the bases of palm leaves and cocking its head to inspect crannies in the bark. Insects are hidden in there—juicy centipedes, weevils, and grubs—but many of them are out of reach, buried deep in the vegetation or curled up at the bottom of wormholes drilled into the tree trunks.

An ordinary bird might be stymied by these difficulties, but not our crow. Without hesitation, it flies to a nearby tree and picks up a twig that it had left there a few minutes earlier. At first glance, the stick doesn't look particularly special: it's just a sprig from a native deciduous tree, *Elaeocarpus dognyensis*, that has been stripped of leaves and bark. On closer examination, however, you can see that the stump-end of the twig, where the crow snapped it off the branch, has been nibbled to form a tiny hook. And watch what the crow can do with it! Grasping the twig in its bill, the bird flies directly back to its foraging site, positions the stick so that one end is braced against the side of its head, and then deftly inserts the implement, hook first, into the crevice. With a few quick flicks of its beak, the bird works the twig back and forth, then pulls it out, with a tasty insect squirming on the end of it. Crow, the Tool User, in action.

This techno-savvy bird is a New Caledonian crow, *Corvus moneduloides*, a species found only on the remote islands of Grande Terre and Maré in Melanesia. (New Caledonia is a French colony about a thousand miles northeast of Brisbane.) When the bird's sophisticated tool behavior was first described by biologist Gavin Hunt of the University of Auckland, New Zealand, in 1996, the news made headlines in the prestigious journal *Nature* and raised a hitherto little-known species to celebrity status. And as the spotlight fell on the New Caledonian crow, the glow of scientific fascination quickly spilled out to include all the other species of crows around the world.

How Crow PERFECTED *the Spear*

✦ ✦ ✦

According to the myths of the Aborigines of Australia, there was a time long ago when two great beings, the Eagle and the Crow, were in conflict with each other. Both hunted with spears, but only the Eagle knew how to make spearheads with backward-pointing barbs, which would stay in to make the kill. The Eagle tried to protect its secret, but one night, when everyone else was sleeping, the Crow took the Eagle's spearhead out of its hiding place and had a good look at it. From then on, the Crow was able to make barbed spearheads and kill its own kangaroos.

▲ *Raven design from a Viking scabbard mount.*

They're out there in our own backyards, spying on us from lampposts, steal-ing food from the dog, and shattering the early morning with their loud, steel-edged caws. If one species of crows routinely makes and uses tools—a behavior so remarkable that it was until recently thought to be uniquely human—then what might the rest of those swaggering, black-clad wise guys be up to?

CROWS OF THE WORLD

There are about forty-five species of crow in the world (a couple more by some estimations, a couple fewer by others, depending on whether local vari-eties are split into separate entities or lumped together). Although they are known by a variety of common names, including ravens, jackdaws, and rooks, all are members of the genus *Corvus*, or crow, and all are variations on a theme, with their glossy black (or sometimes black-and-white) plumage, their rau-cous voices, and their seemingly endless capacity to fly out of the frame of our expectations and surprise us. They are medium-sized or largish birds—the smallest, the European jackdaw, *Corvus monedula,* is about the size of a large cockatiel—with sturdy bills, strong feet, and venturing minds that are formed for exploration and discovery. The burliest member of the crow tribe, the common raven, *Corvus corax,* is as big and brassy as a macaw and just as im-

◅ *From left to right, the carrion crow, the common raven,*
and two African species, the pied crow and the thick-billed raven.

pressive, with its liquid calls, rustling cape of feathers, and keen alertness. (One of the most widespread birds in the world, the common raven is found throughout the Northern Hemisphere, from Europe and North Africa east through Asia and across the northern reaches of the New World.)

In between these extremes in size lie the other members of the global crow congregation, including a dozen species found exclusively in Europe and Asia—among them the gregarious rook, *Corvus frugilegus,* a familiar bird of farmland across both continents, pied hooded crow, *Corvis cornix,* and its all-black cousin, the carrion crow, *Corvus corone.* Another eight or nine species are native to Africa, and five or six are found only in Australia: the Australian raven, *Corvus coronoides,* for example, with its mournful, fading wail, and the only-slightly-smaller little crow, *Corvus bennetti,* which is famous for its exuberant aerial displays. Yet another dozen-plus species are unique to islands in the South Pacific and the West Indies, from New Caledonia and New Guinea to Jamaica.

Strangely, there are no crows at all in South or Central America, where *los observadores de pájaros* have to be content with a profusion of brightly colored jays and magpies, the crows' closest relatives. (Crows, magpies, and jays belong to different genera, or kinship groupings, within the larger family connection of the tribe Corvini.) North America is blessed with four species all its own: the sociable northwestern crow, *Corvus caurinus,* of the west coast; the glossy fish crow, *Corvus ossifragus,* of the eastern seaboard, with its distinctive nasal caw; the heavyset Chihuahuan raven, *Corvus cryptoleucus,* of northern Mexico

➢ *In this illustration by Arthur Rackham, the mythic*
ravens Hugin and Munin drift over the mountains of Valhalla.

and the southwestern United States; and the lively American crow, *Corvus brachyrhynchos*, which is seen and heard almost everywhere else. Rounding out the clangorous chorus, in North America as elsewhere in the Northern Hemisphere, is the common raven, which drifts over gloomy forests and bleak tundra from sea to sea to sea, uttering its sonorous commentary.

Crows and ravens make a statement just by being themselves. Everything about them says, "It's me. I'm here. This is my world, my place in the world, and don't you forget it." They are the opposite of shyness, the antithesis of camouflage, the very embodiment of self-promotion. And although their showy behavior is primarily intended to attract the attention of others of their kind, their "advertising package" is also ideally pitched to attract the human ear and eye. Unlike the little dickey-birds that set us scrambling for binoculars and frantically twiddling knobs, crows are big and bold, making them easy to observe and identify. As a rule, individual species of *Corvus* are not difficult to tell apart, if you spend a few minutes learning their particular field marks. The common raven, for example, can be distinguished from all the other crows that share its range by its large size; its big schnoz, or heavy bill; its slotted wing tips; and its diamond-shaped, rather than fan-shaped, tail.

Even the crows' harsh voices are—if not exactly music to our ears— surprisingly companionable. Technically speaking, crows are songbirds, though you wouldn't know it from what comes out of their mouths. Not for them a soaring aria that would put the Three Tenors to shame. Instead, crow

vocalizations are earthy, studded with what sound to us like consonants and vowels, as if their caws and "quorks" were pronouncements in some unintelligible tongue. And this attunement between humans and crows, this resonance, is both striking and unexpected. Why the connection between bird and mammal? For whatever reason, crows stir our senses, and, over the centuries, their harsh calls have echoed loudly through our dreams and myths. When the legendary Crow or Raven speaks, even the gods listen.

GHASTLY, GRIM, AND ANCIENT RAVEN

In ancient Greece, the raven was celebrated as the sacred bird of Apollo, god of healing, prophecy, and the sun. But even familiars of the gods can get into trouble. As Ovid tells us in his *Metamorphoses*, it seems that Apollo once had a lover named Coronis, the prettiest girl in all of Thessaly, though not, alas, the most chaste. One day, Apollo's Raven—at that time a splendid, silver-white bird—caught the girl in *flagrante delicto* and, "merciless informer" that he was, flew straight to his master and shouted out what he had seen. Boiling with Olympian rage, Apollo picked up his bow and arrow and shot Coronis through the breast, then almost immediately succumbed to regret. Unable to save his lover, he turned on Raven instead, the fatal loudmouth that had uttered a truth better left unsaid. As punishment for this lapse of discretion, Apollo banished Raven from the company of white birds, which is why, to this day, ravens are black as night yet bright as the sun's rays.

In Norse mythology, ravens had the ear of the warlike Odin, the father of the gods. Having traded one of his eyes for a sip at the Well of Wisdom, Odin relied on his black henchmen, the ravens Hugin and Munin, to fly through the nine worlds and return at night to his throne, bringing him whispered news of everything that was going on. Often the news was bloody—Munin means "memory," especially memory of the dead. And ravens were also associated with the gruesome Valkyries (from Old Norse *valkyrja* and Old English *waelcrige*, the raven, or "chooser of the slain.") Not only did the ravening corpse goddesses flock to the scene of battle, but they could also see into the future, foretell the outcome of the combat, and determine which of the warriors were doomed to die. The Irish war goddess Badb performed the same bloody services, in the guise of either a raven or a carrion crow.

Crows and ravens are scavengers, which is a polite way of saying that they eat the dead, so it is darkly fitting that they were linked to the carnage wrought by swords and war axes. In India, by contrast, the pretty little house crow, *Corvus splendens,* is a bird of the domestic scene, found around virtually every human habitation in the country, even in the center of crowded cities. Perhaps the only species of bird that is entirely dependent on humans for its habitat, the house crow has been living communally with people for hundreds of years, feeding on garbage, nesting in treed gardens, and performing aerial stunts off the tops of tall buildings. But house crows are also found on the burning grounds, where the dead are laid on their funeral pyres for cremation.

DEMON BIRD

❖ ❖ ❖

During the witch craze in Western Europe, ravens and crows were sometimes feared as demons. In Strathnaver, Scotland, for example, in the seventeenth century, an entire congregation of prayerful souls was seized with dread when they sensed a spectral raven in the house with them. Evil emanated from this shadowy presence, and the people were paralyzed with fear. A day passed and then another, and the group decided to sacrifice the householder's son to the bird spirit. And so they would have done had it not been for the intervention of a servant. Eventually, neighbors rallied to tear the roof off the house, and the raven's dire spell was broken.

↟ *Common raven, as pictured by Rev. F.O. Morris*
in his A History of British Birds, *1851.*

As an intimate presence in both life and death, the crow is revered in India as an evocation of the ancestors and is respectfully fed both at times of bereavement and during an annual period of remembrance called Shraadh.

What if it is true that the crows hopping around on the boulevard embody the memory of the beloved dead? Or more portentous yet, what if in their dark shining they represent the mystery at the very heart of existence?

In Native communities around the Northern Hemisphere (particularly the northwest coast of North America and eastern Siberia), people cherish the living tradition of a spirit Raven, or sometimes a spirit Crow, which imparted its irreverent and ribald spirit to the world. A rapscallion of the first order, with no regard for decorum or sentiment, this great Raven created humans and then, more or less whimsically, condemned them to death. According to a tradition of the Tlingit people, recorded in writing in Wrangell, Alaska, in 1909, Raven made two attempts to produce humans, once out of rock, a project he abandoned because it was too slow, and once from a leaf, an easy-to-use material that suited him better. "You see this leaf," he said to his new creations. "You are to be like it. When it falls off the branch and rots, there is nothing left of it." That is why people die, the elders said, because

*◄ Mrs. Stene-Tu and her son, members of the
Tlingit Raven Clan in southeastern Alaska, were photographed
in their potlatch dancing costumes around 1900.*

Raven had made them from leaves that perish. According to the Australian Aborigines, by comparison, the great Crow created death because he wanted to have his fun with the widowed women.

But if Raven was opportunistic and often thoughtless, he was not malicious. He did the best he could for his new creations. Through trickery, theft, and seduction, he provided his people with everything they needed for survival: daylight, fire, rivers full of salmon and eulachon—even the knowledge of how to make love. The lusty Raven was only too happy to provide a demonstration. His spirit was so much like a person's that he could transform himself into a human whenever he wished and pass himself off as a baby or a member of the opposite sex, usually with dire and twisted consequences. When Raven was on the scene, loved ones died under questionable circumstances, and precious possessions disappeared. And if his misdeeds were often wryly hilarious, his frailties were also unsparingly recognizable. But perhaps it is not surprising that the Raven and his people had so much in common, since each had created the other in his own image.

REVOLUTIONS IN EVOLUTION

Seen with the transforming eye of the imagination, the crows and ravens of mythology resemble people in fancy dress, a noisy and good-naturedly venal tribe of avian superheroes. But what happens when we consider the genus *Corvus* with the cold, hard gaze of science? Is there any factual basis for positing a special kinship between crows and humans?

> ➤ *Birds are thought to be the direct*
> *descendants of flying, feathered reptiles.*

At first glance, the evolutionary evidence does not looking promising. According to the paleontologists, birds and mammals are the products of two distinctly different branches of the tree of life. Their most recent common ancestor was a vaguely amphibianlike creature that lived in the swampy tropical forests of the late Carboniferous Period, at least 280 million years ago. At that point, the most advanced life-forms on the planet were aquatic or semi-aquatic organisms, such as fish and frogs, that were obliged to spend all or part of their lives in water. The progenitors of birds and mammals, by contrast, produced eggs with hard, mineralized shells that could be laid right out on dry land and thus marked an early, tentative step in the conquest of terra firma.

From that imponderably distant starting point, evolution followed two divergent paths. One lineage—known as the Synapsida, or "beast faces"—eventually gave rise to the earliest mammals, furry, scurrying, shrewlike creatures that appeared on the scene about 220 million years ago, during the late Triassic Period. Meanwhile, the other line—the Sauropsida, or "lizard faces"—evolved into all manner of reptiles, notably, the dinosaurs. Birds either descended from some anonymous reptilian ancestor and evolved alongside the mighty dinos (as witness a fragmentary but seductively birdlike fossil from Texas called *Protoavis*, which dates to about 225 million years ago) or else, as most experts contend, are descendants of the great beasts themselves (as witness the delicate fossil remains of feathered dinosaurs, dating back some

150 million years, that were recently discovered in China).

No matter how this question is eventually answered, one fact is clear: the evolutionary gulf between birds and mammals is almost incomprehensible. This conclusion comes as a surprise to those of us who grew up on biology textbooks in which the members of the classes Aves and Mammalia were typically presented together as warm, fuzzy creatures that, despite their differences, were each other's closest living relatives. But with insights gained from an ever-improving fossil record and advances in genetic analysis, taxonomists have recently begun to emphasize not the kinship between the two groups but their disjunction. As the only surviving members of the synapsid lineage, mammals are placed in a class by themselves, but birds are now listed as a subgrouping of the reptiles: the class Aves in the clade, or evolutionary line, of Reptilia. And if it is true that birds—crows among them—are just glorified lizards, then what is the chance we could have anything significant in common with them? Perhaps the connection that we sense with crows and ravens is nothing but wishful thinking, an expression of our own deep yearning for intelligent company.

But remember that life, like the mythic Raven, has a few tricks up its sleeve and is not to be stymied by mere improbabilities. Just as evolution can

RAVEN MAKES THE FIRST PERSON

✦   ✦   ✦

ABRIDGED FROM *THE WORDS OF AN UNALIT, OR YUP'IK,*
STORYTELLER IN COASTAL ALASKA, AS RECORDED IN THE 1890S

It was in the time [the elders said] when there were no people on the earth. During four days the first man lay coiled up in the pod of a beach-pea (*L. maritimus.*) On the fifth day, he stretched out his feet and burst the pod, falling to the ground, where he stood up, a full-grown man. He looked about him, . . . and he saw approaching, with a waving motion, a dark object which came on until just in front of him. . . . This was a raven, and, as soon as it stopped, it raised one of its wings, pushed up its beak, like a mask, to the top of its head and changed at once into a man. . . .

At last he said: "What are you? Whence did you come? I have never seen anything like you."

To this Man replied: "I came from the pea-pod." And he pointed to the plant from which he came.

"Ah!" exclaimed Raven, "I made that vine, but did not know that anything like you would ever come from it."

⋏ *The face of a Yup'ik boy, with raven tattoos, 1890s.*

start with a single ancestral life-form and take it in different directions to produce wildly different results, so too can those divergent end points gradually converge, or begin to resemble one another. The power of flight, for example, has arisen at least three times from three evolutionary beginnings, in insects, reptiles, and mammals. Bees, birds, and bats are all airborne today because, through eons of time, their assorted ancestors responded independently to the opportunities and challenges of taking to the sky. Life is infinitely transmutable, and it is entirely normal and unexceptional for organisms from widely separated branches of the evolutionary tree to bend together and acquire similar characteristics. Does this kind of evolutionary convergence account for the connection between crows and humans? If it does, how alike have we two become? And why would anything so unlikely ever have happened?

CROW UNIVERSITY

The ability to make and use tools has long been considered a hallmark of intelligence and one of the distinctive characteristics of human beings. ("The first indications that our ancestors were in any respect unusual among animals," writes physiologist Jared M. Diamond in his book *The Rise and Fall of the Third Chimpanzee*, "were our extremely crude stone tools that began to appear in Africa by around two-and-a-half million years ago.") And it is certainly true that tool use is a rare and remarkable achievement in the living world. For example, of the roughly 8,600 species of living birds, only about 100 have ever been known to drop a shell on a sidewalk, batter prey against a wall, or do anything else that could even remotely be considered technological. If the scope of the discussion is narrowed to include only "true tool use"—the manipulation of objects that are held in foot or beak and used to accomplish a task—the number of species that qualify drops by more than half. By this definition, the list includes only such *rara avis* as the Egyptian vulture, which occasionally uses stones to hammer ostrich eggs, and various species of chickadees and tits, which sometimes use twigs to probe into crevices.

The only name to show up time and again on the list of tool-using birds is *Corvus*. For example, there is a report from Oklahoma of an American crow that tore a sliver of wood off a fencepost, placed it under its feet, and pecked at the tapered end as if to shape the point. The bird then used its tool to poke into a narrow hole where a spider was hiding. In Scandinavia, carrion crows have been known to tug up ice-fishing lines, holding the tangled line with their feet between pulls and then flying away with whatever they can steal from the hook. And in the city of Sendai, Japan, members of this same species have learned to use cars as nutcrackers. The crows perch at controlled intersections, and when the cars stop on red, the birds swoop down and place the hard-shelled nuts in the path of the traffic. After the cars have moved through, the birds fly down to feed or, if the nuts are still intact, to reposition them for another try.

FOR THEIR SIZE,

{ C R O W S }

are among the B R A I N I E S T organisms

on Earth, *outclassing* not only other

B I R D S *(with the possible exception of parrots)*

but also most M A M M A L S.

• • •

◄ In this extraordinary photograph by researcher
Gavin Hunt, a wild New Caledonian crow uses a stick tool
to investigate a crevice in a tree trunk.

But most impressive of all is the New Caledonian crow, one of perhaps two nonhuman species—the other possibly being the chimpanzee—in which *all* individuals in *all* populations routinely make and use simple technology. (The roster of toolmaking animals also includes orangutans, African and Asian elephants, and the woodpecker finches of the Galapagos, but their tool use is restricted to geographically defined groups.) New Caledonian crows are also exceptionally versatile toolmakers, producing not just one but several kinds of implements. In addition to making probes from twigs, both with hooks and without, they also manufacture finely crafted "stepped" tools from the stiff leaves of the pandanus tree. Working delicately with the sides of their bills, clipping and tearing by turns, the birds cut out shapes that look like half of a skinny Christmas tree as seen in a child's drawing. One side is left straight, while the other is cut to a sharp point at the top and then widened out in steps toward the bottom. This design combines a fine tip for probing with a broad base for stability and ease of handling. As a final touch, the birds also ensure that natural barbs found along the straight side of the leaf-tool curve downward from top to bottom so that they can be used to rake insects out of crevices.

How do mere birds create such intricate artifacts? Are the crows mindless robots, programmed by their DNA, or could they really be as smart as they seem to be? Or perhaps they are genetic-brainiac combos, with both an innate talent for toolmaking and a mental bent toward design and invention. Nobody knows for sure. But researchers have discovered that, for their size, crows are among the brainiest organisms on Earth, outclassing not only other birds (with the possible exception of parrots) but also most mammals. In fact, the brain-to-body ratio of a typical crow is similar to that of a chimpanzee and not far off our own. And just as we and other primates have a large prefrontal lobe, the presumed seat of our higher intelligence, so crows also have exceptionally large forebrains that may serve a similar function. Could it be that the evolutionary challenges that encouraged our own ancestors to amass all those little gray cells also pushed the ancestral crows to grab a brain for themselves?

At Oxford University in England, a team of scientists led by zoologist Alex Kacelnik has recently begun to investigate these provocative questions. As a first step, the researchers have established a captive colony of New Caledonian crows in their laboratory and are designing experiments to test the birds' understanding of basic physics. To date, the star of this project is Betty, a young female crow who was caught in the forests of Grande Terre island, New Caledonia, in March of 2000. Once settled into her new accommodations—a room with a large outdoor aviary that she shared with another crow, called Abel, a male of unknown age who was acquired from a New Caledonian zoo, Betty quickly began to show the world what she could do.

In one series of trials, for example, she was presented with the challenge of obtaining food—pig's heart, her favorite—by poking a stick through a small hole in a plug. The trick was to insert the stick through the hole and

The **C R O W** and the Pitcher

✦   ✦   ✦

FROM *AESOP'S FABLES*, SIXTH CENTURY BC

A thirsty Crow found a Pitcher with some water in it, but so little was there that try as she might, she could not reach it with her beak, and it seemed as though she would die of thirst within sight of the remedy. At last she hit upon a clever plan. She began dropping pebbles into the Pitcher, and with each pebble the water rose a little higher until at last it reached the brim, and the knowing bird was enabled to quench her thirst.

Moral: Necessity is the mother of invention.

⋏ *"Little by little does the trick" in this drawing by Richard Heighway, 1896.*

use it to push a food cup along a tube to a downward elbow bend, where the cup would fall out onto the table and the food could be eaten. Provided with several tools of different diameters, including some that were too large for the hole, Betty always chose the smallest one available. She did so even if her pesky keepers tied up her preferred tool with a bunch of other sticks, just to make things more interesting. Not once did she select a tool that was too big to fit. And when she was provided with a branch from an oak tree and allowed to manufacture tools for herself, she almost always produced probes that were the right size for the task. If the hole in the plug was large, she produced large sticks; if the hole was narrow, she kept on whittling.

In another experiment, both Betty and Abel also demonstrated an understanding of length. Given a selection of tools to choose from, some too short to reach the cup, they usually picked out a stick that was long enough. In twenty trials, Betty made the wrong choice on only five attempts, and Abel scored an impressive 95 percent. But the most exciting experiment of all was one that the crows set up for themselves. In this case, food had been placed in a little bucket at the bottom of a transparent tube, from which it could be re-

◄ *This fifteenth-century Hungarian*
coat of arms features a crow brandishing a twig.

moved only by reaching down and snagging the handle of the bucket with a hooked tool. A selection of wires was provided for the birds, some straight (and therefore presumably useless) and some hooked (just right for the task), and the researchers stood by to see how the birds would respond. In the first few trials, everything went as expected, as the crows sized up the situation and figured out what to do. But in the fifth run-through, Abel added an unexpected variation by picking up the only hooked tool in the room and flying away with it, leaving Betty with nothing to work with but a straight length of wire.

Although Betty had often been given wire tools to use, she had never made them herself and had never even had an opportunity to see wire being bent. Nonetheless, she flew over to the tube and peered at the food from various angles. Then, in less time that it takes to describe it, she picked up the wire, stuck one end under a piece of tape at the base of the apparatus, and, pulling back with body and bill, bent it into a hook. Down the tube it went, through the handle, and voilà, dinner was served. When the researchers recovered from their amazement, they ran a series of trials in which Betty was challenged to repeat her accomplishment, and, although she did not always produce perfectly rounded hooks, she always succeeded in bending the wire and hoisting up the food. The great Raven himself couldn't have done it better. No other animal—not even a chimp—has ever spontaneously solved a problem like this, a fact that puts crows in a class with us as toolmakers.

TWO

Family

DRAMAS

✦   ✦   ✦

NIMALS CAN DO amazing things without so much as a thought. Spiders spin webs that are marvels of geometry and finesse. Wasps build elaborate multichambered nests to shelter larvae that they skillfully feed and tend. Even the lowly squid produces clouds of ink and deploys it tactically when threatened. Yet so far as anyone knows, neither arachnid nor insect nor mollusk ponders deeply before it responds, weighing the options and considering pros and cons. The animal just does what it does, and, in a very literal sense, the rest is history. Although many organisms can modify their responses slightly through personal experience, most inherit their basic menu

➤ *In this fantastical portrait of Napoleon I, a golden*
hand commands his shoulder, a spider spins a web across the
map, and a crow emerges from the emperor's hat.

of behaviors from their ancestors. What used to be known as "instinct" is now ascribed to the entwined, encoded complexity of genetics. Generally speaking, the ability of animals to fine-tune their responses—to behave appropriately in particular circumstances—is a reflection not of intelligence (no matter how smart the behavior may look) but of the versatility and intricacy of the double helix.

But if genetics alone can equip an animal to deal with life's challenges, why bother getting smart? Evolution is a ruthless master; innovations that don't pay off are left behind in the fossil beds, and the evolutionary advantages conferred by intelligence are not always obvious. Compared with a surefire reflex that has been tested for generations, thinking is uncertain and time-consuming. (There is no survival benefit in figuring out what to do after the tiger has pounced on you.) So why did sophisticated intellectual abilities develop? What were the circumstances in which the ability to create a mental model of the world began to pay off in improved survival and increased reproduction?

For the last several decades, scientists have been racking their own brains to find answers to these questions. They have wondered, for instance, if tool use might have motivated the development of mental powers. In the end, however, the theoreticians have concluded that this is putting the cart before the horse and that tool use is likely a result of intelligence rather than its cause. In other words, when animals like crows and humans make

tools, they are probably employing mental capacities that originally evolved in response to some other, even more difficult and basic challenge.

Nothing is more intellectually challenging than living in a social group, surrounded by a bunch of other animals that are sharpening their wits on you. To live long and prosper, a social animal needs a full array of mental defenses, including the capacity to recognize, remember, anticipate, analyze, and think strategically. Accordingly, most scientists now believe that higher intelligence likely arose in intensely sociable species where individuals could gain an evolutionary upper hand through their interactions with one another. If this supposition is correct, it implies that intelligent species are likely to live in complex societies. We know this is true for humans, but could it be so for crows? Smart as they are, they're only birds, and it hardly seems credible that a jazzed-up reptile could maintain a network of interpersonal relationships or assess shifts in social conditions and adapt to them. But then a crow is not your average featherhead.

N O T H I N G

is more INTELLECTUALLY challenging

than living in a SOCIAL group,

SURROUNDED by a bunch of other animals

that are sharpening their WITS on you.

✦   ✦   ✦

CATCHING CROWS

Biologist Carolee Caffrey is madly in love with corvids. Over the last twenty years, she has studied the social behavior of American crows in California, Oklahoma, and Pennsylvania and has come away from her research with a joyful respect for the bright minds of her subjects. Yet even though it is the birds' intelligence that makes her work so much fun, she would be the first to admit that their edgy alertness causes complications. To study crow society, you first have to be able to tell the birds apart so that you can chart family relationships and keep track of how individuals interact with one another. But to do so, you have to catch them—ideally every bird on the study site—and fit each one with an identification tag. "The only way to catch crows is to trick them," Caffrey laments, "and it's such an ordeal that it prevents most sensible people from studying them."

Of all the methods she has tried over the years (nooses of monofilament line sewn into Astroturf, which the birds wouldn't land on; glue traps that wouldn't hold their feet; walk-in traps that the crows wouldn't walk into; and so on), the most successful has been a device that shoots a net out over a flock of crows that has been lured to a food bait. Because crows become more wary of the apparatus with every attempted capture, the trick is to attract several birds into range at once, thereby increasing the chance of catching them before they all catch on to the setup. And it can't be just any old group of crows in the shot; you have to wait for the ones you want, the unmarked birds that have so far avoided getting caught. It is not a job for the faint of heart.

The scene: a park in Stillwater, Oklahoma. The time: the darkness before dawn. An old Ford Explorer pulls up to a stand of trees; the doors open, and a crew of researchers spills out. Working quietly so as not to attract attention, they sweep away a pile of leaves that has sat there for the past two weeks, set up their net launcher in its place, drape the equipment with camouflage material, and throw leaves back over top. Even the wire that runs from the net to the detonator in the car is tucked into the bushes and covered up. To human eyes, everything looks exactly the same as it had the day before, when the unmarked members of a local troop of crows were hopping all over the lawn, greedily feeding on the cooked spaghetti, dry cat food, and other delicacies laid out to entice them.

Morning comes and with it the family of crows. But before the birds can land and feed on their breakfast buffet of pizza and hard-boiled eggs, one young male apparently notices something out of the ordinary. He flies directly over the path of the "hidden" wire and follows it to the car. Flicking his eyes toward the windshield, as if to see who is waiting there, he then sounds a loud alarm. Caw, caw! Danger! The whole family immediately flees from the trap and never returns. "My students and I have spent hundreds of hours planning and preparing trapping attempts, and thousands of hours waiting in cars," Caffrey ruefully admits, "yet we remain the undeniable runners-up in this battle of wits." At best, she expects to succeed on one of three attempts.

The odds are considerably better if you can mark birds in the nest, before they are old enough to put up much resistance. But that too calls for a person

UNCATCHABLE

✦　　✦　　✦

According to a story in Ovid's *Metamorphoses,* there once was a virgin princess, a girl so beautiful that she attracted the attention of the lecherous sea god, Poseidon. When sweet words failed to seduce her, the hot-blooded Poseidon attempted to take her by force, and the girl called to the heavens for help. Her plea was answered by the virgin Athena, goddess of wisdom and war, who turned the vulnerable princess into a hard-to-catch crow.

"I was stretching out my arms to the sky," Crow says, in Ovid's telling; "those arms began to darken with soft plumage. I tried to lift my cloak from my shoulders but it had turned to feathers with roots deep in my skin. I tried to beat my naked breast with my hands but found that I had neither hands nor naked breast."

Once airborne, Crow escaped with her virtue intact and entered Athena's service.

⌄ *As wings sprout from her shoulders, Coronis, or Crow, flees from the lecherous Poseidon.*

who can rise to the challenge. Although American crows have been known to nest in shrubs or even on the ground, they generally prefer high-rise accommodations. Nests are typically located in the upper branches of a tall deciduous tree or, more often, a conifer, anchored to stout branches, in close to the trunk, and obscured by dense, dark, prickly cover. According to Kevin McGowan, another of the fearless few who study American crows, the birds seem to appreciate a room with a view. "I'll go into a backyard here in Ithaca, New York," the city where he works, "and think it's just another tree. But when I climb up to the nest, it turns out that, from way up there, the crows can see the lake. It's amazing how often the nests have a wonderful vista."

Fortunately, for X-treme birders like McGowan, getting there is half the fun. A few years ago, he remembers finding himself at the top of a crow-nest tree, a tall white spruce with brittle branches and a divided top. "There I was, a good 18 meters [60 feet] above ground," he recalls, "with one foot on each trunk, measuring nestling crows. It was a windy day and things were really whipping around. I looked down at the ground and thought, 'I am getting zero adrenalin out of this. Is that a good thing or a bad thing?' I'm still not sure." But when friends tell him that he needs a new hobby, he doesn't listen to them. Catching crows is not a pastime for him. "We're working to

≺ *A frog, sitting in a gutter, talks its way out of being*
eaten by a crow, in this illustration of a Tibetan folktale.

understand the social behavior of an extraordinarily common bird about which surprisingly little is known," he says. "We're trying to get something accomplished."

TO HELP OR NOT TO HELP

The ties that bind in a family of birds generally do not bind for long. Although mates often form long-lasting relationships—pairs of crows, for example, may remain together for years or until parted by death—parents and their offspring usually associate with one another for only a few months. As soon as the young are able to fend for themselves, they fly away, never to be seen again, in an annual reenactment of the empty-nest syndrome. (Curiously, female birds generally move farther afield than young males do, reversing the dispersal trends that are typically seen among mammals.) This pattern is found in at least 95 per cent of all living birds, including many species of crows—the majority of common and Australian ravens, for example, as well as fish crows, jackdaws, and rooks, among others.

But what keeps the researchers hard at work are the exceptions to the rule, the 2 or 3 percent of bird species that routinely breed in cooperative, family-based groups. Because crows are so ridiculously hard to study, nobody knows exactly how many species belong in this category, but the number is expected to keep growing. New Caledonian crows, for example, are probable candidates for inclusion, though these birds are so elusive—shimmering shadows

➤ *This array includes, from left to right, eggs
of the common raven,* Corvus corax; *carrion crow,* C. corone;
hooded crow, C. cornix; *and rook,* C. frugilegus.

that melt into the darkness of the tropical canopy—that they are difficult to
see, much less to study. So far, after a dozen years of effort, biologist Hunt and
his small band of intrepid jungle explorers have found only a handful of nests.
So much for understanding the birds' social behavior! Yet the researchers are
intrigued by the interactions they glimpse at feeding stations, where juveniles—young of the year that are clearly capable of feeding themselves—
nonetheless beg from adults, presumably their parents, who obligingly cough
up food for them. This observation suggests that, even after they attain independence, juvenile New Caledonian crows may stay with Mom and Dad, a
behavior that strongly suggests a cooperative system.

In general, cooperative breeding occurs when young birds delay dispersal
(and thereby forgo the opportunity to mate and produce young of their own)
in favor of remaining with their parents and helping out around home.
And this eccentric behavior is not restricted to exotic South Sea islands;
it can also be observed in backyards and parks in many parts of Canada
and the United States. Thanks largely to the Herculean efforts of Caffrey,
McGowan, and their co-workers over the past dozen years, we now know
that cooperative breeding is common—though not universal—among
American crows. Across the northern plains, for example, in a region that includes the Canadian prairies but that has not yet been conclusively mapped,
the crows appear to breed as independent pairs, without the assistance of
helpers. Elsewhere on the continent, by contrast, although some pairs breed

COUNTING **CROWS**

✦   ✦   ✦

OLD ENGLISH RHYME

One crow sorrow,
Two crows joy,
Three for a girl,
Four for a boy,
Five for rich,
Six for poor,
Seven for a witch,
I can tell you no more.

⋏ The Seven Ravens, *by A. Weisgerber, 1905.*

as independents, a significant percentage of broods are attended by retinues of three, six, ten, or even a dozen crows, mostly the grown-up offspring of the breeding pair.

Some of these so-called helpers never contribute much and seem to be freeloading off their parents. But others pitch in, whether by standing guard over the family territory, helping to chase intruders away, bringing food to the female on the nest, or feeding nestlings. "I have observed helpers literally following in their parents' footsteps," Caffrey reports, "sitting next to and watching their parents during nest building, being thwarted by breeders as they attempted to feed nestlings inappropriate items, and jostling with the breeding female for a chance to brood eggs and nestlings, something she never lets them do." Perhaps the helpers are parents-in-training, acquiring skills that they will later use in rearing their own broods, though there is as yet no evidence that this speculation is true. Crows that have served as helpers are no more successful in fledging young on their first independent breeding attempt than those that have no prior experience.

LIFE STORIES

The benefits of cooperative breeding, whether for the helpers or their folks, are still a matter of conjecture. And if the whys of the situation are perplexing, the hows—the way in which each individual youngster decides what to do—are even more wonderfully mystifying. Somehow, each young crow in a

CROW TEMPERAMENT

✦   ✦   ✦

▲ A family of young crows roosts "in a row, like the big folks,"
in this drawing by Ernest Thompson Seton, 1898.

FROM "INDIVIDUALITY, TEMPERAMENT AND GENIUS IN ANIMALS,"
BY ROBERT M. YERKES AND ADA W. YERKES, *NATURAL HISTORY*, APRIL 1917

The experimenter who ignores individuality or temperament in his subjects runs a grave risk of misunderstanding or wrongly evaluating his results. Our descriptions sound anthropomorphic, but that, the alert reader will appreciate, is due to our avoidance of stilted and unnatural terminology. We are attempting to describe in an intelligible way, and briefly, behavior which, if we should restrict ourselves to wholly objective terms, would require pages of unusual behavioristic statement.

Among the birds, there is probably no more interesting object of study than the crow. . . . One summer we removed a brood of four young crows from their nest just before they were able to fly. . . . Our space will not permit us to recite in detail, as we are tempted to do, the peculiarities which these birds exhibited during that memorable summer. We must content ourselves with the simple statement that in reactions . . . of wildness, fear, timidity, curiosity, suspicion, initiative, sociability, the individuals differed most obviously and importantly. We hope sometime, in justice to the problem of crow temperament, to devote a summer to the intensive study of sex and individual differences in these extremely intelligent birds.

◄ *Squealing and straining with hunger,*
three carrion crow chicks appeal to their parents for food.

cooperative population chooses among an open-ended range of options. In any given brood, one individual (likely a female) may disperse permanently to join a family miles down the road and thereafter return at most for an occasional visit. Meanwhile, another may leave for weeks or months and then come back home to live and even to assist its parents. Another (typically a male) may stay put for a year or two or longer, either helping or just hanging out, before eventually moving in with the next-door neighbors and becoming a member of that group.

By human standards, crows don't live for long: the oldest wild bird on record died at age fourteen, and most are lucky to make it past their seventh birthday. But within that brief compass, they pack in life histories full of adventure and unexpected twists. For instance, McGowan remembers a young female that he marked as a nestling in Ithaca who was later sighted at a bird-feeding station 10 miles out of town. By the following week, she was back in her natal territory, helping her parents, and she stayed with them through that breeding season. The next summer, however, she flew back out to the country, where she mated and settled down before dying the following year.

"I can't help but think that she noticed her male while she was out exploring," McGowan says, "thought, 'Hey, that guy's cute,' and then came back later to see if his female had died. Lo and behold, he was available, and there you have it."

And lest anyone is discombobulated by this attribution of human thoughts and motivation to a bird, McGowan is happy to admit that he

49

> ➤ *A carrion crow, as pictured by Rev. F.O. Morris*
> *in his* A History of British Birds, *1851.*

doesn't know how crows make their decisions. But do they go prospecting for opportunities? Meet other individuals? Remember the crows and places they've been? Do they consult these memories when making decisions about where to live and with whom? Without doubt, they do. If the behavior of crows and humans sometimes invites similar descriptions, it is not necessarily a sign of anthropomorphism, McGowan insists, but of fundamental similarities between two intensely social animals.

This is a conclusion that Carolee Caffrey seconds with enthusiasm. She has, however, noticed one important difference between crows and us: their families are generally more peaceful than ours sometimes are. No matter what the provocation, family members usually work out their differences without violence or any other signs of overt aggression. For instance, in 2001, near the campus of Oklahoma State University in Stillwater, there lived a family of crows that included a breeding male and female, their two-year-old son, his two year-old brothers, and a one-year-old sister. The breeding female died that summer, and, by fall, a new female had turned up to take her place. Life went on without incident until it was time to breed, when both the father crow, known as XT from the markings on his tags, and the oldest son, NK, began to court the female. One day XT would be sitting right beside her, preening and being preened, and the next time it would be NK who was billing and cooing. This went on for two whole weeks, without any sign of strife. Then one morning, XT was gone, and that very afternoon, NK and the female,

now his new mate, started
to build a nest together.

A week passed, and x t
was nowhere to be seen.
Meanwhile, the family on
the neighboring territory
was experiencing troubles
of its own. First, a one-year-
old daughter, the only helper, was killed by a great horned owl; then the breeding male was struck by a car. The only survivor, the mother, was left with a nest
full of young and no one to help her care for them. Days passed, and the female beat back and forth, carrying food to the nest. Then suddenly, there was
x t again, on the roof beside the tree, right in the heart of the widowed bird's
territory. That in itself was unusual, since crows usually stay out of each
other's domains, but what happened next was downright astonishing. With a
casual flick of his wings, x t drifted down to the nest and tenderly placed food
in the mouth of one of the orphaned young.

According to classical evolutionary theory, x t's act of apparent kindness
should never have happened. If the purpose of life, crudely stated, is to ensure the survival of one's own genes, then it is a mistake to help raise anyone
except your brothers and sisters or, better yet, your own progeny. The neighbor's chicks, so far as anyone knows, were not related to x t. Could it be that,

having been eased out of his own territory by his upstart son, he decided to help the widow next door as a part of a long-term plan to reestablish himself as a breeding bird? If so, his strategy was successful, for he and his new female bred together the following year and raised a brood of three before his disappearance and probable death late in the summer. Such are the subtleties of crow society.

THE PLOT THICKENS

The American crow, as its name suggests, is restricted to the New World, but a very similar corvid spreads its wings across Europe and Asia. The carrion crow is one of the most widespread and, in some localities, abundant birds in the world, with a range that extends through half a dozen subspecific variations from the North Sea south to the Mediterranean and from Ireland east to China and Japan. Until recently, the birding community thought it had the species pegged as a noncooperative breeder, with no capacity for the complexities of helping. But this certainty was disrupted in 1995 with the discovery of a population of carrion crows in the province of León in northern Spain, in which 75 percent of the territories are occupied by cooperative family groups. "It is such a striking pattern, so easy to see, that I was very surprised that nobody had noticed it," says researcher Vittorio Baglione, who made the find with collaborators from Sweden, Italy, and Spain. "It is almost impossible to see just two crows flying around together. There are almost always more." The largest group on record had nine members.

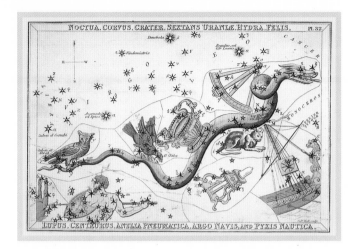

Nest DEFENSE

✦   ✦   ✦

PARAPHRASED FROM *THE PANCHATANTRA*, A COLLECTION OF STORIES
PUBLISHED IN INDIA BETWEEN AD 200 AND 400

Once upon a time, a crow couple built a nest at the top of the tree. Unfortunately, a serpent lived at the base of this very same tree, and it used to crawl up and steal all the crows' eggs. The crows were deeply grieved by this and, when it happened time and again, they called on their friend the jackal to help them come up with a plan.

The jackal advised the crows to steal something valuable from the king and throw it into the serpent's burrow. So the male crow went to the palace and stole a necklace from the queen while she was bathing. The palace guards followed the crow all the way back to the tree, where they discovered the gems in the reptile's den. They promptly killed the serpent and recovered the necklace. Now the crows were happy because they had protected their family from danger.

⋏ *According to the ancient Greeks, the god Apollo banished the raven to the constellation Corvus after the bird tried to blame his own misdeeds on Hydra, the water serpent.*

As in North America, each family lives year-round on an exclusive territory. Although individuals may step out briefly to join a temporary flock at
the garbage dump or to sleep at a communal roost, group members spend
most of their time and meet most of their needs on the family *propiedad*. Not
surprisingly, each group defends its holdings against invaders, which are ex-
pelled with vigorous chases and a machine-gun fire of caws. But if the in-
comer is an older sibling that has dispersed and returned to visit for the
afternoon, the residents greet it quietly and permit it to forage with them.
Baglione suspects that the birds recognize family members that they have
lived with in the past and are therefore able to distinguish between unwel-
come intruders and welcome guests.

Carrion crow society is built on a web of male friendship. Females apparently disperse outside their family networks (and beyond the study

◄ Carrion crows gather to feed in snow-covered
fields on the outskirts of a village, in this illustration
by German artist Walter Georgi, 1902.

perimeters), but the males typically stay home with their parents for a year or two before scouting the neighborhood for a new place to live. By analyzing DNA from tagged crows, Baglione and his team have been able to show that dispersing males usually settle with their male relatives, perhaps birds they know from personal experience. (In one instance, a yearling checked out two territories, visiting each twice, before moving in with an older brother that had dispersed in the previous year.) So potent a force is brotherly love that both males often copulate with the one breeding female in the group, each fertilizing some of the clutch and giving new depth to the term "cooperative."

The question remains: How do they do it? How does a bird brain negotiate all these intricate social moves? Wouldn't it be easier to believe that crows are clever robots, acting out a complex set of genetic instructions? To test this possibility, in 2001, Baglione and his collaborators transferred eggs from a mom-and-pop population in Switzerland, where helping is unknown, to the cooperative Spanish population, and vice versa. When Spanish chicks fledged in Switzerland, they immediately dispersed from their natal territory and joined temporary flocks of juveniles, just like all the other Swiss birds. But when Swiss crows grew up in Spain and were reared by cooperative family groups, five of the six surviving crows stayed home and became helpers. This pretty much lays to rest the idea of a simple genetic explanation and opens up new vistas for thought and speculation.

THREE

The Trickster

REVISITED

◆   ◆   ◆

T HE COMMON RAVEN is not, so far as anyone knows, an especially family-oriented bird.
There is only one report of cooperative breed-
ing in this species: a yearling raven in Minnesota that quixotically decided to
stay home for an extra summer, guard its younger brothers and sisters in the
nest, and occasionally accept feedings from its parents. As a rule, however,
young ravens progress toward independence at a breakneck pace. In the few
weeks between hatching (which occurs in early April to mid-May, depending
on latitude) and fledging (mid-May to mid-June), a clutch of naked, floppy

➤ *A raven in all its splendor calls to both*
eye and ear. This color engraving, by R. Havell,
is based on a drawing by John J. Audubon.

pink gargoyles is miraculously transformed into a handsome brood of flapping, squawking, fully feathered juveniles. By July or August, these enterprising youngsters will have flown off their parents' territory and set out to fend for themselves, at the ripe old age of four or five months.

Yet even after they make the break with home, these young vagabonds are not completely cut adrift from the company of other ravens. As the poet John Donne might have put it, had he been a bird-watcher, no raven is an island, entire of itself. Although a newly independent raven may pass its days alone, scouting the land for food, it is likely to spend the nights crowded in with dozens or even hundreds of its fellows at a communal roost. The largest roost on record, on a power transmission line in southwestern Idaho, attracted as many as 2,103 noisy, jostling ravens. It's a kind of all-night party, attended by different birds on different nights, with frequent shifts of location, depending on the food supply. According to data from radio-tracking studies, each bird appears to operate independently, coming and going at will, as part of a complex and fluid network of acquaintances.

It may be here, in these avian nightclubs, that young ravens meet prospective mates and try out their courtship displays: jittery, dancelike routines of bowing, gurgling, knocking, fanning, tail spreading, and head fluffing. By age two, the birds may have chosen their lifelong partners, though they are not likely to reproduce until their third or fourth summers at the earliest. (One bird on record did not breed until his seventh year.) From then on, the members of the pair spend most of their time on their territory, an area of between roughly 2 and 20 square miles that they occupy year-round and defend vociferously against other ravens. At night, partners typically roost near one another, often in the same tree, and often take time to preen each other, "kiss" with half-opened bills, and hold one another's feet. On occasion, however, even these devoted homebodies fly off to sleep at a communal roost if the weather is severe or to join the greedy crowd that gathers to feast on a dead deer.

But just because ravens spend time with one another doesn't mean they're all sweetness and light. This is a species, remember, that is known in myth and legends from around the world as something of a rogue, and that spirit of malfeasance—that rascally inclination to prosper at another's expense—also inflects the interactions of real-life ravens. The same female that snuggles up to her mate at night may sneak away the minute his back is turned and copulate with a neighbor. A juvenile feeding on a carcass may roll onto its back when other ravens fly overhead—as if to say, "I'm dead, guys; don't risk it"—and then right itself and resume feeding when the potential competitors have left. (This behavior was noted by a trapper in central

RAVEN *gets his* WAY

✦   ✦   ✦

AN ABRIDGED VERSION OF A STORY TOLD BY A TLINGIT MAN
FROM WRANGELL, ALASKA—A MEMBER OF THE RAVEN CLAN—IN THE EARLY 1900S

Raven saw a whale out at sea and he wanted to bring it into shore. So he took a knife and some fire-making equipment and flew into the whale's mouth. For a time, he lived inside the whale, eating fish and the whale's meat, but after he cut out the whale's heart, the beast died and started to drift. Raven then sang his magic songs to bring the carcass onto a sandy beach, where his calls attracted the local people. When they cut the whale open, Raven escaped and flew off into the woods, crying "Q!one', q!one', q!one'."

Raven stayed away long enough for the people to render the whale's fat into oil, boxes and boxes of it. When he returned, he pretended not to know what had happened. Where had the whale come from? he asked. Had the people heard a noise when it came ashore? Yes, they said, they had heard strange sounds and seen a dark shape flying away. "Years ago just such a thing as this happened," Raven told them, "and all of the people who heard the noise died. You people must leave right away. Don't eat anything. Leave it here." So all of the people ran away, and Raven took all the oil.

⤊ Raven (Hooyeh) in Whale (Koone), *by Haida artist Johnny Kit Elswa, 1883.*

Saskatchewan and reported with a note of caution by biologist Bernd Heinrich in his 1995 book, *Mind of the Raven.*)

Scheming and deception by animals are hot topics in contemporary science. If higher intelligence is a response to the challenges of living in social groups, then brain power should pay off in improved mastery of social situations. Individuals should gain a survival advantage—more food, more sex, longer lives, increased reproduction—by using their brains to outwit and outmaneuver their friends and associates. Put bluntly, this theory predicts that exceptionally smart animals will also be exceptionally tricky. With this provocative idea in mind, a small but gleefully determined band of researchers has begun to look for proof that ravens and other bird brains not only connive and scheme but that they know exactly what they are doing.

RAVEN ALLIANCES

On a wintry afternoon in October 1984, researcher and marathon runner Bernd Heinrich made a simple observation that, over the next four years, would engage both his mental and his physical skills. He was at his cabin in western Maine when all of a sudden he heard a hullabaloo of raven cries echoing through the forest. A good mile away, he discovered a group of ravens shouting around a moose carcass. If he had been attracted by the commotion, he thought, surely other ravens would have been drawn to the food source as well. "The birds seemed to be advertising their find," he noted, "which meant they would have to share it." But this behavior didn't seem to make sense. Why didn't the noisy ravens just shut up and eat the moose themselves?

As this question took hold of his mind, Heinrich hatched a plan: he would drag carcasses into the forest and watch to see what happened. Over successive winters, he distributed more than 135 piles of meat in the Maine woods, for a total of almost 8 tons, including 3 road-killed deer, 5 moose, 3 cows, 12 calves, 2 sheep, 3 goats, innumerable loads of slaughterhouse offal, and numerous carcasses of small mammals. To prevent coyotes from stealing his baits, he took the precaution of peeing on them, such was his dedication to science. Then, as each offering was put in place, he established an observation post—in a cabin, in a blind, or in dense branches at the top of a tall spruce—and crept into place each morning an hour before dawn so that he could watch the ravens without disturbing them. In all, he spent 1,520 hours making observations.

By the time Heinrich climbed down from his tree for the last time, two general patterns had emerged. When ravens fed on carcasses, they either showed up in ones and twos and scarcely uttered a sound, or else they arrived in congregations of two or three dozen birds, amid a hubbub of raucous calls. By capturing and marking individuals, Heinrich was able to show that the singletons and pairs were adult, mated birds on their territories, whereas the noisy crowds consisted mainly of wandering youngsters. Why the difference?

The T H R E E Crows

◆　　◆　　◆

A VERSION OF THE OLD ENGLISH BALLAD "THE THREE RAVENS,"
AS SUNG IN THE CAROLINAS IN THE 1880S

There were three crows sat on a tree,
And they were black as they could be.

Said one old crow unto his mate,
"What shall we do for something to eat?"

"There lies a horse on yonders plain
Who's by some cruel butcher slain

"We'll perch ourselves on his backbone,
And eat his eyeballs one by one."

↖ *An Arthur Rackham illustration for "The Twa Corbies,"
or two crows, a Scottish version of the same ballad.*

When a lone juvenile landed at a carcass, it was likely to be attacked and chased away by the resident pair, but not so if it showed up with a group. The young ravens found strength in numbers.

And that wasn't all. It turned out that these gangs of young toughs did not assemble by chance; the ravens actively recruited one another. Heinrich concluded that a special, high-pitched yell uttered by juveniles at carcasses attracts others to the scene and that together the mobs of young ravens are able to descend and feed. In a later set of experiments—inevitably involving the recovery and transportation of another few hundredweight of road kill—he and his colleagues demonstrated that feeding crowds also develop out of communal roosts. Hungry youngsters, eager to feast on something dead, follow the lead of birds that know of a nearby carcass.

Yet even after all these exertions, there was one problem Heinrich still couldn't crack. When ravens form these shifting alliances, do they consciously plot and scheme, or are they acting on impulse, without thinking? And the same tantalizing perplexity hangs over another aspect of the ravens' social repertoire. In addition to associating strategically with one another, the birds strike up pragmatic relationships with wolves and other large carnivorous mammals. Long the subject of excited speculation, the wolf-raven partnership was conclusively documented in 2000 by Daniel Stahler, one of Heinrich's graduate students. As a member of the team responsible for monitoring the reintroduction of wolves to Yellowstone National Park, Stahler

> In his collection of fables, LaFontaine tells the story of "le Renard,"
> the fox, who tricked "le Corbeau," the crow, into dropping a round of cheese.
> In reality, however, neither crows nor ravens are easily deceived.

spent several winters following radio-collared packs and watched them make more than two dozen kills. In almost every instance, the predators were accompanied by a retinue of black hangers-on, which hovered overhead or perched on nearby rocks. On the five occasions when ravens were not present at the moment of death, they arrived on the scene within four minutes.

The ravens were purposefully following wolves; that much was obvious. But Stahler and his colleagues also caught a glimpse of an even wilier permutation of the relationship. The ravens sometimes led the wolves to carcasses. (Since ravens cannot slice through animal hides and open bodies, they rely on wolves to do the dirty work for them.) One winter day in 1999, six wolves from a group known as the Druid Peak pack were spotted traveling along one of their regular routes in a snow-covered valley bottom. Overhead, silhouetted against the sky, a cluster of three dozen black, winged forms wheeled in lazy circles. Suddenly, the ravens veered away from the pack and landed some distance off, beside a mound in the snow. Two minutes later by the clock, the lead wolf turned off the well-worn path and, with the rest of the pack in tow, plowed through deep drifts until it reached the spot where the ravens were. There the wolves uncovered a dead elk calf, presumably the same animal that earlier had been seen in the area, injured and bleeding, surrounded by a dark cloud of ravens. Once the carcass had been opened, the ravens landed warily among their wolves, and the co-conspirators fed at the same table.

Le Corbeau et Le Renard

The SAME female

that SNUGGLES up to her mate

at night may *sneak away*

the MINUTE his back is turned

and COPULATE with a neighbor.

•　•　•

MEANWHILE, BACK IN THE LAB. . .

Are ravens tricky? No doubt about it. Do they exploit their social relationships for personal gain? Absolutely. But do they do so intentionally, with full
malice aforethought? That is a much more difficult matter. Yet Heinrich, for
one, is persuaded that the issue of raven consciousness has to be addressed in
the interest of human understanding and good science. "I didn't start out at
all interested in the question of intelligence," he says. "It was forced upon me
by the ravens."

The idea for a raven IQ test came to Heinrich serendipitously, from an article in a children's magazine. Tie a lump of food to a string, the author suggested, suspend it under a perch, and see which birds are clever enough to get
it. This experiment required such minimal effort (no carcasses to lug) that
Heinrich decided to try it on his backyard research colony of captive ravens.
The prize would be a lump of leathery old salami, suspended in midair. The
only way to get it was to pull it up, something these ravens had never done;
Heinrich was almost certain they would be flummoxed. So imagine his as-
tonishment when one raven first cautiously checked out the setup and then
confidently proceeded to pull up loop after loop of string, anchoring each
with his foot, until he succeeded in hoisting up the treat.

In subsequent trials, a few ravens proved unable to solve the problem, an
indication that playing string games is not instinctive. But others—perhaps
the Einsteins of the raven race—obtained the meat within thirty seconds of

➤ *Nature red in tooth and claw—a raven pecks*
at a moose that was injured by a
pack of wolves in Denali National Park, Alaska.

touching the apparatus. Even more amazing in Heinrich's eyes was the fact that the successful birds never flew away with their salami-on-a-rope, as they would inevitably have done with any ordinary morsel. It was as if they understood, without even having to try, that the food would be ripped out of their bills if they attempted to fly. "The significance of the remarkable behavior of *not* flying off was that it was a *new* behavior that was acquired without any learning trials," Heinrich says. "They acted as though they had already done the trials. The simplest hypothesis is that they had—in their heads."

Heinrich's results strongly suggest that ravens are able to think before they act. But there is a big difference between understanding relatively simple physical concepts—meat tied down—and assessing subtle and ever-changing social relationships. And so the mystery persists: do ravens use their smarts to outsmart one another?

CACHE AND CARRY

As a verb, the word "raven" means "devour greedily," and that is exactly what a mob of ravens does when it falls upon a carcass. Any fellow feeling that existed among gang members when they assembled quickly dissolves into a *sauve qui peut* of unabashed self-interest. Each bird attempts to monopolize as much of the meat as it can by tearing off extra bits and hiding them. There is a flurry of rustling wings as ravens come and go, throat pouches bulging with food and bloody scraps of flesh dangling from their bills. Every tidbit is cached separately, often in snow or dirt, and only the bird that hid the food

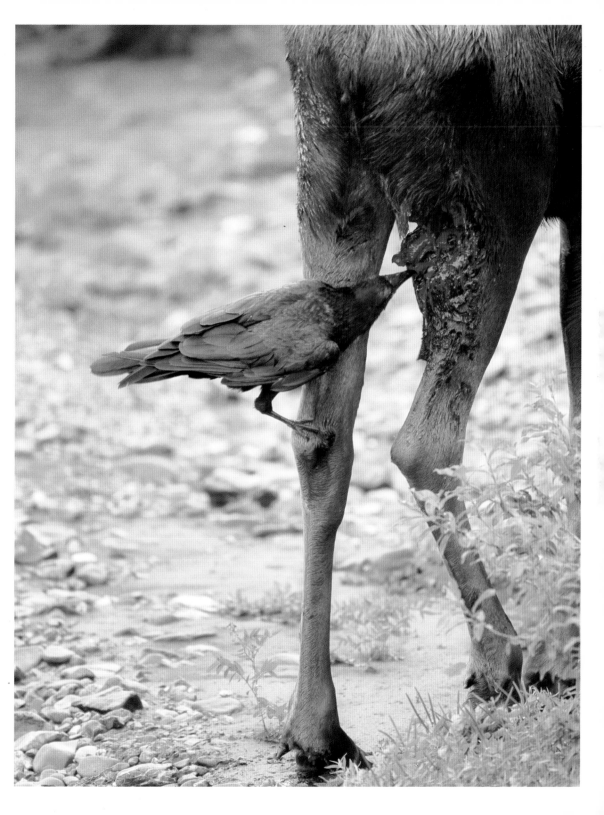

FROM *WILD ANIMALS I HAVE KNOWN*, BY ERNEST THOMPSON SETON, 1898

One day while watching I saw a crow crossing the Don Valley [in Toronto] with something white in his beak. He flew to the mouth of the Rosedale Brook, then took a short flight to the Beaver Elm. There he dropped the white object, and looking about gave me a chance to recognize my old friend Silverspot [an old crow that could be recognized by a white patch on the side of his face]. After a minute he picked up the white thing—a shell—and walked over past the spring, and here, among the docks and the skunk-cabbages, he unearthed a pile of shells and other white, shiny things. He spread them out in the sun, turned them over, lifted them one by one in his beak, dropped them, nesting on them as though they were eggs, toyed with them and gloated over them like a miser. This was his hobby, his weakness. . . . His pleasure in them was very real, and after half an hour he covered them all, including the new one, with earth and leaves, and flew off. I went at once to the spot and examined the hoard; there was about a hatful in all, chiefly white pebbles, clam-shells, and some bits of tin, but there was also the handle of a china cup, which must have been the gem of the collection. That was the last time I saw them. Silverspot knew that I had found his treasures, and he removed them at once; where I never knew.

✦   ✦   ✦

➤ *Crows feast on the remains of the*
unfortunate John Stevens, who in 1635 was hanged,
drawn, and quartered for treason.

knows where to find it—with one critical exception. If another raven happens to be watching, it too will mentally map the spot, intent on sneaking
back and stealing the reward.

This interaction, in which the parties stand to profit by deceiving one another, provides a perfect natural laboratory for studying the mind of the
trickster. If ravens really do attempt to outwit one another in this game of
hide-and-seek, then both parties should be expected to behave strategically.
On one side of the equation, for instance, a bird with food to hide might fly
away from the crowd before burying its treasure or slip behind a boulder,
where it knows it can't be observed. And if, despite these maneuvers, it happens to catch another raven looking, it should dig up its cache and relocate it
to a new and more secure location. Sure enough, in experiments by Heinrich
and his colleagues—notably, Austrian zoologist Thomas Bugnyar—caching
ravens have been found to employ all these tactics. What's more, ravens have
also been known to make "false caches" by going through all the motions of
caching in front of other birds and then, when the would-be thieves rush in,
carrying the food away to hide it in private.

On the other side of the equation, the larcenous observers have a trick or
two of their own. Rather than rushing up to see what the cacher is doing, they
act casually and keep a little distance apart, as if they had no interest in what
was going on. All the while, however, they are surreptitiously maneuvering to
keep their sightlines clear and pinpoint the location of the hidden food. And

even after the cache has been completed and the cacher leaves (with many an anxious backward glance), the observers maintain their undercover surveillance. A minute passes, two minutes. Finally, when the cacher seems to have cleared the area, the would-be thieves dash in, in an attempt to empty the cache before its rightful owner can come rushing back.

When Thomas Bugnyar published these findings in *Animal Behaviour* in 2002, he suggested that, based on his observations of caching both in the laboratory and the field, ravens appear to mislead each other intentionally. Yet he still couldn't entirely exclude the possibility that the birds were on autopilot,

RAVEN OPENS THE BOX

⚊ Celestial Ravens, *by Cape Dorset artist Kenojuak Ashevak, 2003.*

PARAPHRASED FROM A TEXT PUBLISHED ONLINE
BY THE ALASKA NATIVE KNOWLEDGE NETWORK, 1995

In the beginning, the elders of southwestern Alaska tell us, the world was in darkness. The most powerful being on Earth was Raven. One day, he learned of a beautiful young woman who lived with her father, a great chief, on the banks of the Nass River. She possessed the sun, the moon, and the stars and kept them closely guarded in carved cedar boxes.

The only way to steal these treasures, Raven knew, was to trick the woman and her father. So he turned himself into a hemlock needle, fell into the woman's cup, and entered her body with a drink of water. Soon she bore a son, whom the chief dearly loved. When the boy (who was really Raven) grew a little older, he pleaded and cried for the box containing the moon and stars. As soon as his grandfather gave them to him, Raven threw them up the smokehole and they scattered across the sky. Although his grandfather was unhappy, he loved the boy too much to punish him for what he had done.

Soon the boy began crying for the other box—the one containing the sun—and again his grandfather gave it to him. Raven played with the box for a long time. Then suddenly he turned himself back into a bird and flew up through the smokehole and out of the house. After a long time, he heard people below him in the darkness.

"Would you like to have light?" he asked them. Then he opened the beautiful box and let sunlight into the world. The people were so frightened that they fled to every corner of the Earth, and that is why Raven's people are everywhere.

✦   ✦   ✦

THE·CROW AND THE·MUSSEL·

acting out a complex set of genetic instructions. Then along came a raven named Hugin.

Named for one of the all-knowing birds that served the Norse gods in Valhalla, Hugin was a perfectly ordinary six-year-old male that had been bred in a zoo and raised, with a companion named Munin and a couple of other birds, in an aviary at the Konrad Lorenz Research Station in Grünau, Austria. As part of an investigation of social learning, the four ravens were presented with three clusters of film canisters, each marked with yellow, red, or blue. Every day, a different one of the color-coded sets of containers was baited with bits of cheese. The idea was to present the ravens with a problem that would take them some time to solve so that the researchers could make observations at their leisure.

In the event, however, Hugin figured out the rule on the first morning of the trials; after finding one empty box in a cluster, he would move on to the next group until he located the boxes that contained bait. His companion Munin, by contrast, couldn't even be bothered to look. Instead, as the dominant bird in a group, he preferred to bide his time until Hugin found the

◄ *In Aesop's fable, a "helpful" crow taught his*
fellow to break a shell by dropping it on a rock and then
swooped down to claim the food for himself.

food; then he would muscle in and gobble up one or more of the tasty tidbits. With Munin now hanging around the food source, poor Hugin was out of luck. The more lids he flipped and the more cheese he found, the more Munin benefited.

Socially subordinate though he was, Hugin was no pushover. On the first afternoon of the experiment, he came up with a countermove. When Munin began to press in on him, Hugin would interrupt his foraging, fly over to one of the unrewarded clusters, and start opening empty boxes. He kept at it, opening and opening, until Munin came to join him; then, as soon as he saw his rival nosing around the wrong cluster, Hugin would dash back to the rewarded boxes and take advantage of his head start to grab a few extra morsels. This behavior went on for a week, until Munin caught on to the ruse and refused to be led astray. Having lost his advantage, Hugin threw a tantrum—"He started throwing containers around," Bugnyar reports—but he soon regained his composure and learned to compensate for Munin's thefts by stealing from the other ravens in the experiment.

Hugin the raven had told a fib and, until he was found out, had gained a tangible personal advantage through misrepresentation. This shady behavior satisfies the definition of "tactical," or intentional, deception and admits the raven to an exclusive club of sociable liars that in the past has included only humans and our close primate relatives. Think of it as the survival of the trickiest.

FOUR

Fellow

FEELING

◆　　◆　　◆

THE ONLY DISTINCTION left standing between other animals and us is our unique facil-
ity with language. All the other accolades that,
over the years, we have claimed for our own species have eventually had to be
shared, first with the higher primates and now with the "feathered apes" of
the genus *Corvus*. Not only has Man the Toolmaker been forced to make
room on his pedestal for orangutans and chimps, but he has also had to accept the crow that is perched on top of his head. By the same token, human
social interactions have turned out to be remarkably similar to those of many

➤ *In this drawing by American illustrator*
Louis Rhead, the great wizard Merlin consults
two sources of wisdom, book and bird.

primates and corvids. And if Hugin's high jinks are anything to go by, it seems that *Homo sapiens sapiens* cannot even claim to be altogether exceptional in the arts of deceit.

Yet the ability to string syllables together in a meaningful, grammatical order—to catch the world in a net of words—continues to stand as an exceptional and quintessentially human achievement. Although you may one day see a crow using a simple tool or a raven playing a trick, you are never going to find a bird with its beak in a book.

This distinction is important, and it reigns unchallenged, so far, though it too has begun to blur around the edges. Without questioning the central premise of human uniqueness, researchers have been trying to understand the way that language is learned, through the *da-da, ma-ma* babble of babyhood. Our close primate relatives do not burble like this—they can grunt perfectly from day one—but crows and other songbirds are much more like us in this regard. As youngsters, songbirds have to practice their vocalizations by listening to other members of their species, without whose example they cannot learn to sing, and then producing outbursts of burbling, free-form warbling known as "plastic song" and "subsong." A young crow, for example, can sometimes be found all alone on a branch, completely self-absorbed, uttering a liquid, rambling medley of soft caws, coos, clicks, rattles, and grating, rusty-gate sounds. To hear it, you might think you had come upon an avian Ella Fitzgerald; the music expresses the same kind of lyricism and joie de vivre.

Improvisation is the hallmark of crow song. According to zoologist and crow musicologist Eleanor Brown, every phrase in these muttered arias is original. Not only are the song elements strung together freely in varying patterns—four coos, followed by two grating rattles, then a caw/rattle hybrid, followed by five caws, or, another time, a single caw followed by seven short coos—but the elements in the series are also modulated. In a sequence of five caws, for example, each note differs from the next in both pitch and duration. And these changeful incantations can spin on for an hour or more as the bird preens its feathers, manipulates objects, stretches, looks around, and socializes with its companions. Within a family grouping, siblings often vocalize together, either by chorusing back and forth or by singing in unison, uttering the same or very similar sounds at the same moment. Sometimes these pairs of crooners cozy up together, a few inches apart, and synchronize both their songs and their gestures.

What these duos are doing, Brown argues, is harmonizing their songs as a mark of friendship, or social affiliation. Each family of crows that she has

QUOTH *the* CORVID

· · ·

⊼ *A French fish peddler*
is ambushed by a noisy mob of crows, 1899.

GREEK PHILOSOPHER
THEOPHRASTUS, CA. 371–286 BC

It is a sign of rain if the raven, who is accustomed to make many different sounds, repeats one of these twice quickly and makes a whirring sound and shakes his wings. So too if, during a rainy season, he utters many different sounds, or if he searches for lice perched on an olive-tree. And if, whether in fair or wet weather, he imitates, as it were, with his voice, falling drops, it is a sign of rain.

H. DOUGLAS-HOME, BIRDMAN, 1977

Rooks were always said to be ominous birds. In the last century there was a rookery near the castle at Douglas, and when my great-grandfather was fairly young he got irritated by their cawing and ordered the keepers to get rid of them, about three hundred nests. An old crone bawled him out for banishing the rooks. "You wait, they'll be back the day you die!" The time came when he was slipping away and suddenly, to his horror, all the rooks came cawing into the trees around Douglas Castle. "God Rooks!" he exclaimed and subsided into his pillows. "That means I'm going to die today." And he did.

INDEED·I·WILL·WED·THEE ׃ A·PRETTY·CREATURE·IS·THE·HOODIE ∼ JHJF

⤏ *In this illustration from* The Lilac Fairy Book, *1919,*
the youngest of three sisters agrees to marry a sweet-talking hooded crow.

studied has its own vocabulary of sounds, some of which—long and short caws and various rattles—they share with other groups, but many of which are idiosyncratic. One family of four American crows, for example, produced a "kek" caw and a high rattle that none of the other crows in the neighborhood used. At least some of their distinctive syllables were learned. In particular, a fledgling known as P acquired two distinctive caws—translated into English as "ark" and "wok"—by imitating the fish crows that often flew overhead (this was in Maryland.) Several months later, P's sister RU began to use the call in her song as well, further harmonizing the family chorus.

Singing has a calming effect on crow interactions, Brown notes. When two family members come into conflict, one of them often begins to sing, instantaneously putting an end to the hostilities. The more song elements any given pair has in common, the more companionable the birds tend to be and the more time they spend socializing and preening one another's plumage. And the reverse also holds true: The fewer shared sounds, the weaker the social link. For instance, when a lovey-dovey pair of sisters was placed in an aviary with an unrelated crow that had a different song, the established twosome completely ignored the stranger. But as soon as the outsider learned to replicate the sisters' distinctive coo calls, they acknowledged her as one of the group and accepted her as a preening partner. To paraphrase the old saying, it seems that crows of a song join the same throng.

➤ *Crows and ravens*
share an intense social awareness.

THE CULTURE OF RAVENS

Given what we know about crows, it is not surprising to learn that their vocal behavior is intensely social. But what if someone were to tell you that about a species in which social partners not only learn calls from one another but also somehow agree on how to use those calls meaningfully? This is the picture that has been emerging over the last twenty-odd years from a study of common ravens conducted by zoologists Peter Enggist and Ueli Pfister, in an area just south of Bern, Switzerland. The research protocol is simple. A cage containing two captive ravens is placed inside the territory of a wild, free-living pair, and the sounds the birds make during the encounter are recorded. Back in the lab, the biologists analyze the recording, tally the number of "call types" used by each bird—a wonderful variety of gurgling, chortling, trilling, knocking, barking, "quorking," and bell-like peals—and then compare the repertoire of these new subjects with the sounds that are already on record.

To date, the researchers have compiled a library of more than 64,000 vocalizations, elicited from 37 raven pairs. From this cacophony, they have distinguished 84 distinctly different calls, and the list continues to grow as each new pair of ravens is added to the choir. Within the limits of their syringeal organs, the birds appear to be free to learn, imitate, and invent, and their collective vocal repertoire is thought to be open-ended. Yet with all these possibilities at their disposal, each individual adult raven has a limited vocabulary

{      }

△ *Poster for a film version of Poe's "The Raven," about 1908.*

FROM *KING SOLOMON'S RING: NEW LIGHT ON ANIMAL WAYS*, BY KONRAD Z. LORENZ, 1952

"Hansl," [*a carrion crow that lived in the Austrian village of Worden*] could compete in speaking talent with the most gifted parrot. The crow had been reared by a railwayman in the next village, and it flew about freely and had grown into a well-proportioned, healthy fellow, a good advertisement for the rearing ability of its foster-father . . . [By taking care of him once at his owner's request,] I found out that Hansl had a surprising gift of the gab and he gave me the opportunity of hearing plenty! He had, of course, picked up just what you would expect a tame crow to hear that sits on a tree, in the village street, and listens to the "language" of the inhabitants . . .

Once he was missing for several weeks and, when he returned, I noticed that he had, on one foot, a broken digit which had healed crooked. And this is the whole point of the history of Hansl, the hooded crow. For we know just how he came by this little defect. And from whom do we know it? Believe it or not, Hansl told us himself! When he suddenly reappeared, after his long absence, he knew a new sentence. With the accent of a true street urchin, he said, in lower Austrian dialect, a short sentence which, translated into broad Lancashire, would sound like "Got 'im in t'bloomin' trap!" There was no doubt about the truth of this statement . . . How he got away again Hansl unfortunately did not tell us.

◆　　◆　　◆

➤ *This image of "Hooyeh," the heraldic raven*
of the Haida people of the Queen Charlotte Islands,
was created by Johnny Kit Elswa in 1883.

of only about a dozen calls. A few of these creakings and groanings are unique to particular individuals, but most are shared with at least a few other members of the broader population. Could it be that ravens learn some of these vocalizations from one another during adolescence, when they hang out together as roost mates and meet in feeding mobs? Suggestively, the calls of juvenile ravens are more diverse and variable than those of adults.

Although no one knows how young ravens acquire their calls, it is clear that the adults can learn new vocalizations from one another. During the Swiss study, for example, one of the captive males picked up three new utterances from a wild male that he visited. In general, it seems that ravens acquire many of their calls from other members of their sex and that some sounds are almost exclusively gender-specific. As a result, male and female repertoires tend to be quite different from one another. These differences are, however, minimized to a certain extent between mates, which often share four or five calls, some of which they probably learn from one another.

And that's when things really get interesting. For not only do the members of each pair have a distinctive vocal repertoire, but they also have their own rules about how the sounds in their collective vocabulary are to be used. For instance, when presented with the cage of captive ravens, one wild female in the Swiss study responded to the intrusion with a short, rasping quack, which her partner typically answered with a guttural honking call. In another pair, by contrast, the female reacted with the same quacking call, but her

mate replied with a liquid "kwa,"
a sound that no other raven
in the study was heard to utter.
His honking call, by contrast,
was used in response to one
of his partner's other calls—
a dactylic triplet (long-short-
short) of harsh, rasping barks. And so it went, through countless permuta-
tions. Although the situation was always the same—a cage of ravens dropped
off in the woods—each pair's response was unique.

The only possible conclusion was that, with the probable exception of a
few basic vocalizations like the begging cry of nestlings and the yell of feeding mobs, ravens' calls do not come with genetically preassigned functions.
Instead, it seems that these clangorous utterances acquire their definition
and meaning in the context of each raven's social experience. Although "rave-
nese" may not be a symbolic language as we know it, neither is it a simple system of signals, a collection of bestial grunts and groans. We're beginning to
catch a glimpse of something beautiful.

CROW EMOTION

If only, just for a day, we could get inside the skin of a crow or a raven. Imagine: settling your mantle of rustling black feathers, taking flight, floating on
languorous wings through the thin air. What would that crow-self see or

THE SEVEN RAVENS

* * *

⋏ Feast of the Seven Ravens, *by Arthur Rackham, 1900.*

PARAPHRASED FROM *CHILDREN'S AND HOUSEHOLD TALES*
BY JACOB AND WILHELM GRIMM, 1812

There was once a man who had seven sons and a much-loved but sickly daughter. Fearing she would die, he sent the sons to get water from the well so that the girl could be baptized. In their eagerness to fulfill his wishes, the boys jostled with one another, and the jug disappeared down the well. They did not know what to do. When his sons failed to return home as expected, the father flew into a temper and said: "I wish the boys were all turned into ravens." Hardly had he spoken when he heard a whirring of wings and looked up to see seven coal-black ravens flying away.

The parents were sad at the loss of their sons but were consoled by the health of their little daughter, who soon grew strong and ever more beautiful. At first, she did not know about her brothers, but eventually she overheard someone talking about what had happened.

And so it was that she set out to rescue them.

Her journey took her through many trials and terrors, including journeys to the sun and moon. Eventually, the morning star gave her a chicken drumstick, which would open the door of a Glass Mountain, where her brothers were held. Alas, by the time she got there, the drumstick had been lost, and she was forced to cut off her little finger and use it to open the lock.

Once inside the mountain, she had to wait for her brothers, the seven lord ravens, to return for their evening meal. Suddenly she heard a stirring of wings and a rushing through the air, and the great black birds appeared. Her loving presence was enough to break the curse and restore the ravens to their human form, and amid much rejoicing, the family returned home.

◆   ◆   ◆

◄ *Young Marion Gaynor*
feeds her pet crow, "Pete," early 1900s.

think or remember? How would its harsh voice reverberate on its own ear? And most mysterious of all, how would it feel? If William Shakespeare was right to suggest that "one touch of nature makes the whole world kin," does that kinship extend to the blustery inner landscape of emotion?

It's hard enough to understand the things that birds and animals do—how they interact, make decisions, and communicate with one another. But the vaporous stuff of feeling almost defies investigation. To date, scientists have been able to demonstrate that crows and ravens express a range of "motivational intensities," from uninterested to maximum arousal. There is, for instance, a graphable relationship between the number of hunger cries emitted by baby crows and the number of minutes that has elapsed since their parents last brought food. The same is true of territorial invasions; the more serious or the more prolonged the threat, the louder and more frantic the vocalizations.

But although these statistics tell us that the birds are probably feeling something, they cannot tell us what those feelings are. Here our best and only guide is intuition. In his 1989 book *Ravens in Winter*, Bernd Heinrich reflects on the unexpected emotional rapport he often senses with his black-winged research subjects. "It surprises me," he writes, "that many of the ravens' calls . . . display emotions that I, as a mammal for whom they are not intended, can feel." When two ravens are tucked up intimately together, they make cooing sounds that sound tender to his ear. When they are in a situation that would

> *The harsh calls of a
> northwestern crow rip through the bright air.*

make him angry, their deep, rasping complaints seem to express anger. In addition, Heinrich believes that he can sense a wide range of other emotions from a raven's voice and body language, including surprise, happiness, distress, bravado, and braggadocio. "Emotions are more 'primitive' than reason," Heinrich notes, "and I presume that many animals have very similar emotions to our own." But the emotional symmetry between corvids and humans is something special.

Kevin McGowan, the crow man of Ithaca, New York, has no doubt that the birds in his studies have feelings, some of which are directed at him. Many of the crows in the city hate him. In particular, he remembers a young male helper crow that he banded on the campus of Cornell University, in a territory that was used by thousands of people every day. The crow would watch the crowds come and go without fury or fuss, but when McGowan showed up under the nest with his binoculars once every three or four months, the crow would raise a ruckus. "He would pick me out from all those people and start yelling and following me around." Thinking that maybe the binoculars were the giveaway, McGowan suited up a friend and sent him out instead, but the crow completely ignored him.

When his study was most active, McGowan gained such a bad "rep" that he couldn't go anywhere in the city without arousing a storm of resentment. "Everybody would join in," he recalls. "I've had as many as seventy-five crows after me at once." As he extended his research onto territories he had never

EMOTIONS are more

"PRIMITIVE"

than REASON, and I presume

that many *animals* have very

similar emotions to our OWN.

BERND HEINRICH

•   •   •

visited, he discovered that the local crows had often been forewarned. "Some of these guys knew me—they'd start to object the minute I showed up—even though I had never knowingly met them." In the end, he got so tired of playing the bad guy that he started to throw peanuts to the crows he met, "in the hope of making a few friends."

ALFRED HITCHCOCK PRESENTS

Carolee Caffrey has a lifetime of crow stories. There was the time she was watching two crows in Encino, California—a year-old male and his father—foraging under a flowering magnolia tree. When the young male's sister flew in to join them, she accidentally dislodged a petal, which landed beside her brother's face and made him jump. His sister watched this happen, turned, inched along the branch to a flower, plucked a petal with her beak, and inched back over his head. Then she leaned forward, dropped the petal right beside him, and made him jump again. Was she just being a pesky little sister?

There have also been more somber moments. In Oklahoma, for example, Caffrey once saw two adult crows, a breeding male and a helper, break away from their group and come back to feed a family member that was terribly injured. "It was sad," she said, "and so tender." Another time, she was observing a nest through a spotting scope when the breeding pair returned to feed their nestlings, only to discover that their nest had been raided by a raptor in their absence. "In all my life, I've never heard such horrible, bloodcurdling

➤ *The house crow of India is "always chaffing, scolding, scoffing,*
laughing, ripping, and cursing, and carrying on about something or other,"
Mark Twain wrote. "I never saw such a bird for delivering opinions."

screams as the crows made at that nest." The male flew away after a minute or two, but the female stayed behind and, for the next four hours (until Caffrey reluctantly left), tended a surviving but injured nestling by nuzzling it, picking up its neck, and preening the side of its head. All the while, the crow uttered mournful-sounding *oohs*.

Caffrey doesn't pretend to know what the bereaved bird felt, though as an onlooker, she herself was moved to tears. And she has even more questions about the remarkable behavior of another female. Remember the story of XT, the male crow near Oklahoma State University that in 2001 was ousted by his son and took up with the widow next door? That widow, known as AM, was a special favorite of the researchers because they never knew what she would think of next. On one occasion, for example, when a climber scrambled up to her nest, she let go at him with a barrage of angry caws and then flew up into the tree above him and proceeded to hammer at a branch. "I could see she was totally pissed," Caffrey says, "and I thought the hammering was a displacement activity," or a way of letting off steam. Instead, AM kept banging away until she broke off a pinecone, which she then picked up, carried into the air, and launched at the head of the intruder. "Direct hit! Bam!" By the time the poor climber was back on the ground, AM had dropped three more pinecone bombs, two exactly on target.

AM had four chicks that spring. When banded, three of them looked healthy and both soon fledged, but the other was sickly and did not flourish.

One day, Caffrey received an SOS from one of her graduate students, Tiffany Weston, who happened to live across the street from AM's nest tree. The little runt was walking around on her lawn. What to do? The researchers knew from experience that if they left the chick on the ground, it would not be long before a dog or cat picked it off. But they were also reluctant to interfere with natural process. As a compromise, Caffrey suggested catching the baby crow, feeding it a meal of dog food, and then lifting it up to safety on a branch.

Even though the crow could not yet fly, that little bird could run, and it led Weston on a noisy chase around, under, and through the bushes. Meanwhile, all the cawing and commotion had attracted the attention of its mother, AM, who was not impressed by the sight of a human pursuing her offspring. Cawing wildly at the top of her lungs, AM flew repeatedly at Weston, with an ominous rush of wings, and landed a solid blow to her head. When Weston fled into the house with the nestling to feed it, AM stared at her through the window and continued to yell.

Once the chick had eaten, Weston brought it back outside and threw it high in a tree, and things calmed down. The next day, however, the youngster

{ }

THE CROW DANCE

✦   ✦   ✦

AN AFRICAN-AMERICAN FOLKSONG RECORDED BY ZORA
NEALE HURSTON IN JACKSONVILLE, FLORIDA, IN 1935. HURSTON DEFINED
FOLKLORE AS "THE BOILED-DOWN JUICE OF HUMAN LIVING."

Oh my Mamma come see that crow
see how he fly!
This crow this crow gonna fly tonight,
see how he fly!
Oh my Mamma come see that crow
see how he fly!
This crow this crow gonna fly tonight,
see how he fly!
Oh my Mamma come see that crow,
CAAAH!
Oh my Momma come see that crow,
see how he fly!

⋏ *Zora Neale Hurston performs the Crow Dance, date unknown.*

still did not seem to be thriving (it hung on for another couple of days before disappearing, presumably dead), and A M again took up her grievance. She renewed her vigil at Weston's window and stalked her from room to room. "It was the spookiest thing," Caffrey recalls. "Tiff would come out of the living room and walk to the kitchen and A M, who had been peering through the living room window, would follow her around." Sometimes A M cawed loudly; at other times, she was eerily silent, just looking and looking. This went on for the next four days, until Weston made a previously planned move to a house in another neighborhood. "It was amazing," Caffrey says. "We liked A M a lot." Sadly for the researchers, she and her family all disappeared in 2003, at the height of a West Nile virus outbreak.

RAVEN'S GREATEST JOKE

It is disconcerting to find so much of ourselves reflected in a feathered reptile: a bird. Disconcerting, but also revelatory. Our kinship with crows reminds us of the irrepressible creativity of evolution, that endless, free-form expression of the miraculous that has shaped all of Earth's beings, including us. In the vernacular of creation, crows and humans are a kind of living pun, two species with different meanings but the same vibration. It's the kind of double entendre that the mythic Raven would have loved, a cosmic witticism that both puts us in our place and raises our spirits. When a crow leaps into the air, our hearts take wing with it and we join in the rowdy revel of existence.

Notes refer to direct quotations only.

18   Raven speaks, from "Tlingit Myths and Texts:
     Myths Recorded in English at Wrangell: 31, Raven,
     Part I." http://www.sacredtexts.com/nam/nw/tmt/
     tmt035.htm.

22   Raven speaks, from Edward Nelson, "The Eskimo
     About Bering Strait," *Bureau of American Ethnology
     Annual Report for 1896–97* 18 (1899), pt. 1, quoted in
     Peter Goodchild, *Raven Tales*, 49, 50.

23   Diamond, Jared M. *The Rise and Fall of the Third
     Chimpanzee* (London: Vintage, 1992), quoted Alex
     Kacelnik, Jackie Chappell, Ben Kenward, and Alex
     A. S. Weir, "Cognitive Adaptations for Tool-Related
     Behaviour in New Caledonian Crows," forthcoming.
     Available online at http://www.cogsci.msu.edu/
     DSS/2004-2005/Kacelnik/Kacelnik_etal_
     Crows.pdf.

29   "The Crow and the Pitcher," from V. S. Vernon Jones,
     trans., *Aesop's Fables* (London: Pan, 1975 [1912]), 23.

37   Carolee Caffrey, personal communication.

38   Carolee Caffrey, "Catching Crows," *North American
     Bird Bander* 26 (October–December, 2001), no. 4: 149.

39   Ovid, *Metamorphoses*, from
     http://www.auburn.edu/~downejm/Ovid/
     Metamorph2.htm#_Toc476707511.

40–41   Kevin McGowan, personal communication.

45   Carolee Caffrey, personal communication and
     "Female-Biased Delayed Dispersal and Helping
     in American Crows," *Auk* 109 (1992): 617.

47   Robert M. Yerkes and Ada W. Yerkes, "Individuality,
     Temperament, and Genius in Animals," from
     http://www.naturalhistorymag.com/editors_pick/19
     17_04_pick.html.

49   Kevin McGowan, personal communication.

52   Vittorio Baglione, personal communication.

53   "Nest Defense," paraphrased from http://members.
     tripod.com/~srinivasp/mythology/storypa7.html.

60   "Raven Gets His Way," from "Tlingit Myths and
     Texts: Myths Recorded in English at Wrangell: 31,
     Raven, Part I." http://www.sacred-texts.com/nam/
     nw/tmt/tmt037.htm.

61–62   Bernd Heinrich, *Mind of the Raven* (New York:
     HarperCollins, 1995), xiv.

64   "The Three Ravens," from Bertrand Harris Bronson,
     The Traditional Tunes of the Child Ballads, vol. 1 (Prince-
     ton, NJ: Princeton University Press, 1959), 309–10.

69   Bernd Heinrich, personal communication.

70   Bernd Heinrich, *Mind of the Raven* (New York:
     HarperCollins, 1995), 319.

73   "Silverspot's Treasures," Ernest Thompson Seton,
     "Silverspot: The Story of a Crow," *Lobo, and Other
     Stories From Wild Animals I Have Known* (London:
     Hodder and Stoughton, n.d.), 71–72.

77   "Raven Opens the Box," based on "Raven Stories by
     the Marshall Journalism Class, Spring, 1995."
     http://www.ankn.uaf.edu/Marshall/raven/
     RavenStealsSunStarsMoon.html.

79   Thomas Bugnyar, personal communication.

85   "Quoth the Corvid," Theophrastus, quoted in Peter
     Goodchild, *Raven Tales: Traditional Stories of Native
     Peoples* (Chicago: Chicago Review Press, 1991), 146.

85   "Quoth the Corvid," H. Douglas-Home, quoted
     in Iona Opie and Moira Tatem, eds., *A Dictionary
     of Superstitions* (Oxford: Oxford University Press,
     1992), 331.

91   "Hansl the Talking Crow," Konrad Z. Lorenz, *King
     Solomon's Ring: New Light on Animal Ways* (London:
     Methuen, 1952), 86–88.

95   "The Seven Ravens," paraphrased from
     http://grimm.thefreelibrary.com/Fairy-Tales/55-1.

97   William Shakespeare, *Troilus and Cressida*
     Act III, sc. v.

97, 98   Bernd Heinrich, *Ravens in Winter* (New York:
     HarperCollins, 1989), 250.

98, 101   Kevin McGowan, personal communication.

101–102, 105   Carolee Caffrey, personal communication.

102   Mark Twain, *Following the Equator: A Journey Around
     the World* (Harford, CT: American Publishing Co.,
     1897), 355.

104   "The Crow Dance," from http://www.lyonsden-
     books.com/html/sorrow3.htm. Hurston's definition
     of folklore, quoted in John Lahr, "Troubled Waters,"
     New Yorker, Dec. 20 and 27, 2004, 183.

PREFACE

SELECTED ONLINE RESOURCES

American Society of Crows and Ravens. http://www.
ascaronline.org.

Crows.net: The Language and Culture of Crows.
http://www.crows.net.

Crow chat group: http.groups.yahoo.com/group/crows.

CROWS AS PREDATORS

Boarman, William I. "Reducing Predation by Common
Ravens on Desert Tortoises in the Mojave and Col-
orado Deserts." U.S. Geological Survey Western
Ecological Research Center, 2002. Available online at
www.werc.usgs.gov/sandiego/pdfs/RavenMgt.pdf.

Marzluff, John M., and Erik Neatherline. "Corvid Response to Human Settlements and Campgrounds:
Causes, Consequences, and Challenges for Conservation." *Biological Conservation.* Forthcoming.

Neatherlin, Erik A., and John M. Marzluff. "Response of
American Crow Populations to Campgrounds in
Remote Native Forest Landscapes." *Journal of Wildlife
Management* 68 (2004): 708–18.

CHAPTER 1

BASIC REFERENCES

Boardman, William I., and Bernd Heinrich. "Common
Raven." *The Birds of North America* 476 (1999): 1–31.

Goodwin, Derek. *Crows of the World.* London: British
Museum Press, 1986.

Madge, Steve, and Hilary Burn. *Crows and Jays.* Princeton,
NJ: Princeton University Press, 1999.

McGowan, Kevin J. "Fish Crow." *Birds of North America*
589 (2001): 1–27.

Snow, D. W., and C. M. Perrins. *The Birds of the Western
Palaearctic.* Oxford: Oxford University Press, 1998.

Verbeek, N. A. M., and R. W. Butler. "Northwestern
Crow." *Birds of North America* 407 (1999): 1–21.

Verbeek, N. A. M., and C. Caffrey. "American Crow."
Birds of North America 647 (2002): 1–35.

CROWS IN MYTH AND LEGEND

Blows, Johanna M. *Eagle and Crow: An Exploration of an
Australian Aboriginal Myth.* New York: Garland, 1995.

Goodchild, Peter. *Raven Tales: Traditional Stories of Native
Peoples.* Chicago: Chicago Review Press, 1991.

Grimm, Jacob and Wilhelm. *Children's and Household Tales.*
http://grimm.thefreelibrary.com/Fairy-Tales/55-1.

Nelson, Edward W. "The Eskimo About Bering Strait."
Bureau of American Ethnology Annual Report for 1896–97
18 (1899), pt. 1.

"Odin by Micha F. Lindemans." http://www.pantheon.
org/articles/o/odin.html.

Opie, Iona, and Moira Tatem. *A Dictionary of Superstitions.*
Oxford: Oxford University Press, 1992.

Ovid. *Metamorphoses.* http://www.auburn.edu/~
downejm/Ovid/Metamorph2.htm#_Toc476707511.

"Raven Stories by the Marshall Journalism Class, Spring,
1995." http://www.ankn.uaf.edu/Marshall/raven/
index.html.

Ross, Anne. *Pagan Celtic Britain: Studies in Iconography and
Tradition.* London: Routledge and Kegan Paul, 1967.

"Tlingit Myths and Text Index." http://www.
sacred-texts.com/nam/nw/tmt/.

"Tradition of Feeding Animals," http://www.india
profile.com/religion-culture/animalfeeding.htm.

"Valkyries, Wish-Maidens, and Swan Maids."
http://www.vikinganswerlady.com/valkyrie.htm.

AVIAN EVOLUTION

Chatterjee, Sankar. *The Rise of Birds: 225 Million Years of
Evolution.* Baltimore: Johns Hopkins University Press,
1997.

Feduccia, Alan. *The Origin and Evolution of Birds.* New
Haven, CT: Yale University Press, 2000.

Padian, Kevin, and Luis M. Chiappe. "The Origin and
Early Evolution of Birds." *Biological Review* 73 (1998):
1–42.

———. "The Origin of Birds and Their Flight." *Scientific
American* 278 (1998), no. 2: 38–47.

TOOL USE BY CROWS

Caffrey, Carolee. "Tool Modification and Use by an
American Crow." *Wilson Bulletin* 112 (2000): 283–84.

———. "Goal-directed Use of Objects by American
Crows." *Wilson Bulletin* 113 (2001): 114–15.

Chappell, Jackie, and Alex Kacelnik. "Tool Selectivity in a
Non-primate, the New Caledonian Crow (*Corvus
moneduloides*)" *Animal Cognition* 5 (2002): 71–78.

———. "Selection of Tool Diameter by New Caledonian
Crows, *Corvus moneduloides.*" *Animal Cognition* 7
(2004): 121–27.

Cockburn, Andrew. "Evolution of Helping Behavior in Cooperatively Breeding Birds." *Annual Review of Ecology and Systematics* 29 (1998): 141–77.

Cristol, Daniel A., Paul V. Switzer, Kara L. Johnson, and Leah S. Walke. "Crows Do Not Use Automobiles as Nutcrackers: Putting an Anecdote to the Test." *Auk* 114 (1997): 296–98.

Emlen, Stephen T. "Evolution of Cooperative Breeding in Birds and Mammals." In *Behavioural Ecology: An Evolutionary Approach,* edited by J.R. Krebs and M.B. Davies, 301–35. Boston: Blackwell Scientific, 1991.

Hunt, Gavin R. "Manufacture and Use of Hook-tools by New Caledonain Crows." *Nature* 379 (1996): 249–51.

———. "Human-like Population-Level Specialization in the Manufacture of Pandanus Tools by New Caledonian Crows *Corvus moneduloides.*" *Proceedings of the Royal Society of London,* B 267 (2000): 403–13. See also Hunt's website at: http://www.psych.auckland.ac.nz/psych/research/Evolution/Gavin.htm.

Hunt, Gavin R., and Russell D. Gray. "Species-wide Manufacture of Stick-Type Tools by New Caledonian Crows." *Emu* 102 (2002): 349–53.

———. "Diversification and Cumulative Evolution in New Caledonian Crow Tool Manufacture." *Proceedings of the Royal Society of London,* B 270 (2003): 867–74.

———. "Direct Observations of Pandanus-Tool Manufacture and Use by a New Caledonian Crow (*Corvus moneduloides*). *Animal Cognition* 7 (2004): 114–20.

Hunt, Gavin R., Michael D. Corballis, and Russell D. Gray. "Laterality in Tool Manufacture by Crows." *Nature* 414 (2002): 707.

Hunt, Gavin R., Fumio Sakuma, and Yoshihide Shibata. "New Caledonian Crows Drop Candle-Nuts onto Rock from Communally-Used Forks on Branches." *Emu* 102 (2002): 283–90.

Kenward, Benjamin, Alex A.S. Weir, Christian Rutz, and Alex Kacelnik. "Tool Manufacture by Naive Juvenile Crows." *Nature* 433 (2005): 121.

Kenward, Benjamin, Christian Rutz, Alex A.S. Weir, Jackie Chappell, and Alex Kacelnik. "Morphology and Sexual Dimorphism of the New Caledonian Crow *Corvus moneduloides,* With Notes on Its Behaviour and Ecology." *Ibis* 146 (2004): 652–660. Available online at users.ox.ac.uk/~kgroup/morphology.pd.

Lefebvre, Louis, Nektaria Nicolakakis, and Denis Boire.

"Tools and Brains in Birds." *Behaviour* 139 (2002): 939–73.

Nihei, Yoshiaki. "Variations of Behaviour of Carrion Crows *Corvus corone* Using Automobiles as Nutcrackers." *Japanese Journal of Ornithology* 44 (1995): 21–35.

Pain, Stephanie. "Look, No Hands!" *New Scientist* 175 (2002): 44–47.

Rutledge, Robb, and Gavin R. Hunt. "Lateralized Tool Use in Wild New Caledonian Crows." *Animal Behaviour* 7 (2004): 327–32.

Weir, Alex A.A., Jackie Chappell, and Alex Kacelnik. "Shaping of Hooks in New Caledonian Crows." *Science* 297 (August 9, 2002): 981. Betty can be seen in action in a video at http://users.ox.ac.uk/%7Ekgroup/tools/tools_main.html.

CHAPTER 2
EVOLUTION OF INTELLIGENCE

Burish, Mark. J., Hao Yuan Kueh, and Samuel S.-H. Wang. "Brain Architecture and Social Complexity in Modern and Ancient Birds." *Brain, Behavior and Evolution* 63 (2004): 107–24.

Dennett, Daniel C. *Kinds of Minds: Towards an Understanding of Consciousness.* New York: Basic Books, 1996.

Emery, Nathan J. "Are Corvids 'Feathered Apes'? Cognitive Evolution in Crows, Jays, Rooks and Jackdaws." In *Comparative Analysis of Minds,* edited by S. Watanabe. Tokyo: Keiko University Press. Forthcoming. Available online at www.zoo.cam.ac.uk/zoostaff/madingley/library/member_papers/nemery/feathered_apes.pdf.

———, and Nicola S. Clayton. "The Mentality of Crows: Convergent Evolution of Intelligence in Corvids and Apes." *Science* 306 (December 10, 2004): 1903–1907.

Kacelnik, Alex, Jackie Chappell, Ben Kenward, and Alex A.S. Weir. "Cognitive Adaptations for Tool-Related Behaviour in New Caledonian Crows." Forthcoming. Available online at http://www.cogsci.msu.edu/DSS/2004-2005/Kacelnik/Kacelnik_etal_Crows.pdf.

COOPERATIVE BREEDING

Baglione, Vittorio. "History, Environment and Social Behaviour: Experimentally Induced Cooperative Breeding in the Carrion Crow." *Proceedings of the Royal Society of London,* B 269 (2002): 1247–1251.

Baglione, Vittorio, Daniela Canestrari, Jose M. Marcos, and Jan Ekman. "Kin Selection in Cooperative Alliances of Carrion Crows." *Science* 300 (2003): 1947–49.

Baglione, Vittorio, Jose M. Marcos, and Daniela Canestrari. "Cooperatively Breeding Groups of Carrion Crow (*Corvus corone corone*) in Northern Spain." *Auk* 119 (2002): 790–99.

Baglione, Vittorio, Jose M. Marcos, Daniela Canestrari, and Jan Ekman. "Direct Fitness Benefits of Group Living in a Complex Cooperative Society of Carrion Crows, *Corvus corone corone*." *Animal Behaviour* 64 (2002): 887–93.

Caffrey, Carolee. "Female-Biased Delayed Dispersal and Helping in American Crows." *Auk* 109 (1992): 609–19.

———. "Feeding Rates and Individual Contributions to Feeding at Nests in Cooperatively Breeding Western American Crows." *Auk* 116 (1999): 836–41.

———. "Correlates of Reproductive Success in Cooperatively Breeding Western American Crows: If Helpers Help." *Condor* 102 (2000): 333–41.

———. "Catching Crows." *North American Bird Bander* 26 (October–December, 2001), no. 4: 137–50.

Canestrari, Daniela, Jose M. Marcos, and Vittorio Baglione. "False Feedings at the Nests of Carrion Crows, *Corvus corone*." *Behavioral Ecology and Sociobiology* 55 (2004): 477–83.

Ignatiuk, Jordan B., and Robert G. Clark. "Breeding Biology of American Crows in Saskatchewan Parkland Habitat." *Canadian Journal of Zoology* 69 (1991): 168–75.

Kevin J. McGowan's website. "So, You Want to Know More About Crows?" http://birds.cornell.edu/crows/crowinfo.htm.

Richner, Heinz. "Helpers-at-the-Nest In Carrion Crows *Corvus corone corone*." *Ibis* 132 (1990): 105–108.

Verbeek, Nicolaas A.M., and Robert W. Butler. "Cooperative Breeding of the Northwestern Crow *Corvus caurinus* in British Columbia." *Ibis* 123 (1981): 183–89.

CHAPTER 3
RAVEN ROOSTS AND RECRUITMENT

Engel, Kathleen A., Leonard S. Young, Karen Steenhof, Jerry A. Roppe, and Michael N. Kochert. "Communal Roosting of Common Ravens in Southwestern Idaho." *Wilson Bulletin* 104 (1992): 105–21.

Heinrich, Bernd. "Winter Foraging at Carcasses by Three Sympatric Corvids, with Emphasis on Recruitment by the Raven, *Corvus corax*." *Behaviour, Ecology and Sociobiology* 23 (1988): 141–56.

———. *Ravens in Winter*. New York: Summit, 1989.

Heinrich, Bernd, John M. Marzluff, and Colleen S. Marzluff. "Common Ravens Are Attracted by Appeasement Calls of Food Discoverers When Attacked." *Auk* 110 (1993): 247–54.

Marzluff, John M., Bernd Heinrich, and Colleen S. Marzluff. "Raven Roosts Are Mobile Information Centres." *Animal Behaviour* 51 (1996): 89–103.

Parker, Patricia G., Thomas A. Waite, Bernd Heinrich, and John M. Marzluff. "Do Common Ravens Share Ephemeral Food Resources with Kin? DNA Fingerprinting Evidence." *Animal Behaviour* 48 (1994): 1085–93.

Stahler, Daniel. "Interspecific Interactions Between the Common Raven (*Corvus corax*) and the Gray Wolf (*Canis Lupus*) in Yellowstone National Park, Wyoming: Investigations of a Predator and Scavenger Relationship." Master's thesis, University of Vermont, 2000.

Stahler, Daniel, Bernd Heinrich, and Douglas Smith. "Common ravens, *Corvus corax*, Preferentially Associate with Grey Wolves, *Canis lupus*, as a Foraging Strategy in Winter." *Behaviour* 64 (2002): 283–90.

RAVEN CACHING AND COGNITION

Bugnyar, Thomas, and Kurt Kotrschal. "Observation Learning and the Raiding of Food Caches in Ravens, *Corvus corax*: Is It 'Tactical' Deception?" *Animal Behaviour* 64 (2002): 185–95.

———. "Leading a Conspecific Away From Food in Ravens (*Corvus corax*)?" *Animal Cognition* 7 (2004): 69–76.

Bugnyar, Thomas, Maartje Kijne, and Kurt Kotrschal. "Food Calling in Ravens: Are Yells Referential Signals?" *Animal Behaviour* 61 (2001): 949–58.

Bugnyar, Thomas, Mareike Stowe, and Bernd Heinrich. "Ravens, *Corvus corax*, Follow Gaze Direction of Humans Around Obstacles." *Proceedings of the Royal Society of London*, B 271 (2004): 1331–36.

Fritz, Johannes, and Kurt Kotrschal."Social Learning in Common Ravens." *Animal Behaviour* 57 (1991): 785–93.

Heinrich, Bernd."An Experimental Investigation of Insight in Common Ravens (*Corvus corax*)." *Auk* 112 (1995): 994–1003.

———. *The Mind of the Raven: Investigations and Adventures with Wolf-Birds*. New York: HarperCollins, 1995.

———."Testing Insight in Ravens." In *The Evolution of Cognition*, edited by Cecilia Heys and Ludwig Huber, 289–310. Cambridge, MA: MIT Press, 2000.

Heinrich, Bernd, and John W. Pepper."Influence of Competitors on Caching Behaviour in the Common Raven, *Corvus corax*." *Animal Behaviour* 56 (1998): 1083–1090.

Savage, Candace. *Bird Brains: The Intelligence of Crows, Ravens, Magpies and Jays*. Vancouver: Greystone Books, 1995.

———."Reasoning Ravens." *Canadian Geographic* 120 (January/February 2000): 22–24.

CHAPTER 4

VOCALIZATIONS

Brown, Eleanor D."The Role of Song and Vocal Imitation Among Common Crows (*Corvus brachyrhynchos*)." *Zeitschrift fur Tierpsychologie* 68 (1985): 115–136.

———."Functional Interrelationships Among the Mobbing and Alarm Caws of Common Crows (*Corvus brachyrhynchos*)." *Zeitschrit fur Tierpsychologie* 67 (1985): 18–33.

Brown, Eleanor D., and Susan M. Farabaugh."What Birds With Complex Social Relationships Can Tell Us About Vocal Learning: Vocal Sharing in Avian Groups." In *Social Influences on Vocal Development*, edited by Charles T. Snowdon and Martine Hasuberger, 98–127. Cambridge: Cambridge University Press, 1997.

Enggist-Dueblin, Peter, and Ueli Pfister."Communication in Ravens (*Corvus corax*): Call Use in Interactions Between Pair Partners." In *Advances in Ethology 32: Supplements to Ethology*, edited by Michael Taborsky and Barbara Taborsky, 122. Berlin: Blackwell Wissenschafts-Verlag, 1997.

———."Cultural Transmission of Vocalizations in Ravens, *Corvus corax*." *Animal Behaviour* 64 (2002): 831–41.

Richards, David B., and Nicholas S. Thompson."Critical Properties of the Assembly Call of the Common American Crow." *Behavior* 64 (1978): 184–203.

Thompson, Nicholas S."Counting and Communication in Crows." *Communications in Behavioral Biology* 2 (1968): 223–25.

———."Individual Identification and Temporal Patterning in the Cawing of Common Crows." *Communications in Behavioral Biology* 4 (1969): 29–33.

WEST NILE VIRUS AND AMERICAN CROWS

Caffrey, Carolee, Shauna C.R. Smith, and Tiffany J. Weston."West Nile Virus Devastates an American Crow Population." *Condor* 107 (2005): 128–32.

Hochachka, Wesley M., Andre A. Dhondt, Kevin J. McGowan, and Laura D. Kramer."Impact of West Nile Virus on American Crows in the Northeastern United States, and Its Relevance to Existing Monitoring Programs." *EcoHealth* 1 (2004): 60–68.

PICTURE CREDITS

Alaska State Library/39-1080/Case & Draper Photograph Collection 18; Tony Angell 25, 36, 68, 100; British Library 14 (Harley 4431), by permission of the British Library; Carl Cook vi, 6, 32, 80, 89; John Eastcott & Yva Momatiuk/National Geographic/Getty Images 71; Mary Evans Picture Library 35, 39, 40, 43, 51, 54, 67, 75, 84, 86, 94; Florence Collection ii, 3, 9, 10, 21, 22, 29, 30, 46, 72, 78, 83, 103; Barbara Hodgson 17; Gavin Hunt 26; Zora Neale Hurston Collection, James Weldon Johnson Collection in the Yale Collection of American Literature, Beinecke Rare Book and Manuscript Library 104; Dennis Johnson, Papilio/CORBIS 48; Library of Congress 4 (LC-USZC4-889), 53 (LC-USZC4-100077), 59 (LC-USZC4-861), 90 (LC-USZC4-8266), 96 Crows (LC-DIG-ggbain-01179); Charles Mason/Getty Images 56; Arthur Morris/CORBIS 63; James R. Page i, 99; Arthur Rackham Collection/Mary Evans Picture Library 13, 44, 64; Franz R. and Kathryn M. Stenzel Collection of Western American Art, Yale Collection of Western Americana, Beinecke Rare Book and Manuscript Library 60, 93; West Baffin Eskimo Cooperative Cape Dorset, Nunavut 76, reproduced with permission of West Baffin Eskimo Cooperative Cape Dorset, Nunavut.